All Your Waves and Billows

All Your Waves & Billows

A Story of Trials, Faith, and Finishing a Translation

Lisa Leidenfrost

COMMUNITY CHRISTIAN MINISTRIES
MOSCOW, IDAHO

Published by Community Christian Ministries
P.O. Box 9754, Moscow, Idaho 83843
208.883.0997 | www.ccmbooks.org

Lisa Leidenfrost, *All Your Waves and Billows: A Story of Trials, Faith, and Finishing a Translation*
Copyright ©2023 by Lisa Leidenfrost.

Cover design by Samuel Dickison.
Cover photo by Max Ravier on pexels.com.
Interior design by Valerie Anne Bost.

Printed in the United States of America.

All Scripture quotations are from the New King James Version®, copyright © 1982 by Thomas Nelson. Used by permission. All rights reserved.

All rights reserved. No part of this publication may be reproduced, stored in a retrieval system, or transmitted in any form by any means, electronic, mechanical, photocopy, recording, or otherwise, without prior permission of the author, except as provided by USA copyright law.

23 24 25 26 27 28 29 30 31 32   9 8 7 6 5 4 3 2 1

To Csaba, whose wise counsel and loving care were truly a "bridge over troubled water" during those years of rough seas. Thank you for always pointing me back up to God, my source of hope.

For You cast me into the deep,
Into the heart of the seas,
And the floods surrounded me;
All Your billows and Your waves passed over me.
(Jonah 2:3)

Contents

	Acknowledgements	xi
	Preface	xiii
	Introduction	1
1	Ghost Town	5
2	Preparing for Our Return	13
3	What a Night!	21
4	Evacuation	31
5	There and Back Again	47
6	Bamako, Mali	53
7	Life in Mali	61
8	Searching for Answers	67
9	Cook Wanted	75
10	The Bakwé Team	83
11	The Final Months	89

12	Moscow, Idaho	101
13	Who Am I?	107
14	Attempting Church	113
15	Trip to Ivory Coast	119
16	At Home	125
17	June Trip	131
18	The Sun Behind the Mist	135
19	A New Old Car	143
20	The Locked Door	149
21	The Answer	155
22	Reflections on Suffering	165
23	Don't Waste Your Trials	171
24	Saying Goodbye	175
25	Grandma's House	183
26	Memories and Microwaves	187
27	The Return	193
28	Noai	199
29	Kellen	207
30	Finished	219
31	The Final Readthrough	223
32	Church in the Village	229
33	The Dedication	235
34	As the Waters Cover the Sea	239
	Epilogue	241
	Appendix: Three Life Stories	247

Acknowledgements

A SPECIAL THANKS TO ALL WHO HELPED me when I was out of commission. First and foremost is Csaba, who held the fort and was my personal counselor. Next is Noai, who cheerfully took over cooking for the family while we were in Africa, and our sons, who willingly took over the chores. A big thanks goes to friends who gave me a cup of cold water through visits and acts of kindness during that time. Last of all, but not least, thanks to my good friend Meredith, who was there again and again when I needed her, especially during those initial hard years. I am truly grateful.

Thanks to Robert Hale, director of the Ivory Coast branch of Wycliffe, for all his help getting us out of Ivory Coast during the unrest, and to the church elders back in Idaho who kept in contact during that scary time.

Thanks to Christ Church for seeing this project through to the finish line of the New Testament and beyond.

On the editing front, a general thanks to those who reviewed this book. A special thanks to Michelle Leidenfrost, my daughter-in-law, who helped at a time when I was almost there, but not quite. Her ability to read a story line and offer input in crucial areas helped me get to the finish line. And thanks to Lisa Just, my editor at Community Christian Ministries, whose editorial skills are phenomenal.

May God bless these people over and over again. We are truly grateful.

Preface

> Therefore we also, since we are surrounded by so great a cloud of witnesses, let us lay aside every weight, and the sin which so easily ensnares us, and let us run with endurance the race that is set before us, looking unto Jesus, the author and finisher of our faith, who for the joy that was set before Him endured the cross, despising the shame, and has sat down at the right hand of the throne of God. (Heb. 12:1–2).

IN THE DARK NIGHT OF SUFFERING, when you don't understand what is going on and you think what is happening to you must be a horrible mistake, you have to hang on to what you know to be true: God's character and the promises in His Word. These promises tell us who He is and where He is going—His glorious plan for bringing in His kingdom.

To know that God is *good* means knowing that good is happening right now in your situation, even in the midst of turmoil. To know that God is *all knowing* and *all powerful* is to believe beyond a shadow of a doubt that everything is under His control. To know that God is *love* is to understand that He has not forgotten you. He is working this trial for your everlasting good. Understanding God's story is knowing that there will be an end to these present sufferings, and that end will be glorious because ultimate victory will come from the Author of all stories.

God is the God of all our death and resurrection stories. Sometimes, to get to the good He means you to have, you have to give up your ideal of what you wanted to happen. The good He intends is not only for you, but for others who will be blessed by your trial. Believing this takes faith, and the growing of faith, although painful, is very precious to God. It is not just a one-time victory; it is a process that bears fruit with each skirmish won along the way. That process is where patience comes in, and leaning hard on the everlasting arms that are *always* there underneath. This is also where faith comes in, faith that believes that God is using all the hardship in our lives to accomplish His ultimate purpose of spreading His kingdom throughout the whole earth. Each painful step along the way is part of this glorious purpose. No trial is ever wasted in His hands.

"For the earth shall be filled with the knowledge of the glory of the Lord, as the waters cover the sea" (Hab. 2:14).

LISA LEIDENFROST
Moscow, Idaho
2023

Introduction

> God moves in a mysterious way,
> His wonders to perform;
> He plants His footsteps in the sea
> And rides upon the storm. (William Cowper)

I SHUT MY EYES AND REMEMBERED THE times we had flown over the Sahara Desert before, where sand dunes drifted lazily in and out of view as we glided over the hot, still land. Csaba[1] and I were missionaries with Wycliffe Bible Translators serving the Bakwé people of the Ivory Coast. We and our four children, Hans, Andreas, Noai, and Jeremiah, had flown this route each time we

---

1. Csaba is a Hungarian given name pronounced *CHAH-ba*.

returned to the West African country. The journey was usually peaceful, but this time was different. As we flew over Mali, we could see storm clouds forming. The horizon grew black with layers of inky folds that billowed up to a massive height and boiled over, spilling murky turmoil across the landscape. In the middle, streaks of lightning illuminated the sinister interior. The scene had a subduing effect on us, as though we were in the presence of a bad-tempered giant. The most disconcerting aspect was that we were flying straight into the giant's jaws.

I felt a foreboding as I watched the storm coming closer, so ominous and silent, and I thought, "Couldn't we go another way? Can I get out now?" I realized there was no way around the storm since it took up the entire horizon.

Over the intercom, the pilot announced the obvious—that we were about to fly through a tropical storm. He added that it would be far worse than expected and ordered us to sit tight. I looked up and saw a young stewardess still serving juice. Flight attendants going about their work are always a reassuring sign, so I took comfort in this until the head stewardess walked up and snapped at her, "The captain wants us to sit down—now."

The juice server replied, "OK, after I do this next person."

The head stewardess shot back, "No! He meant *now!*" It was then that I realized we were in for it.

Within a few minutes, the plane plunged into the mouth of the giant and started to lurch and shake in the darkness.

Knowing how much planes can be jerked around in storms like this, I felt frightened. I have always hated the feeling of a roller coaster plunging up and down; now we were trapped in a hunk of metal in the middle of the air with no way out. I looked out the window, which was a mistake, because I saw the wings bending at an angle I didn't think was possible. I hoped those wings would stay on.

I stole a glance at the children to see how they were faring on this violent horseback ride in the sky. The boys were intently watching their movie. Noai, a few seats away, kept stealing worried glances at her father. Csaba sat there like a calm rock, which reassured Noai, so she settled down to continue her movie as well. I also kept stealing glances at Csaba to get courage. I always looked to him when I was concerned about anything; his calm exterior helped me to focus on the Rock of Ages that never wavers.

As the winds tossed us through blackness streaked with brilliant flashes of light, I was reminded of what helplessness meant, and what trust in God could do. What we didn't know was that this storm was a harbinger of things to come. As we headed back to Africa, we were entering a period of our lives that was to be marked by a series of storms so large that they would have crushed us in their jaws had we not looked to our unseen pilot, our great Lord, to guide us through.

Chapter 1

Ghost Town

ABIDJAN, OCTOBER 2004

It felt good to stand on Ivorian soil again. We got our bags and went through customs, then out the double doors of the airport, where we found our colleague Ambroise waiting for us. As we left the air-conditioned building, we were instantly bombarded by the sounds, smells, and *life* of tropical Africa. Compared to milder places on earth, this environment—replete with colors, brightness, culture, insects, noises, odors, and the vast bustle of humanity—was larger than life. Africa has a way of commanding all the senses and filling them to overflowing—sometimes a good thing, and sometimes not. It happened every time we came back.

On the four-lane highway, cars, trucks, and motorbikes flooded the roads and spilled out into the pedestrian areas. Pedestrians retaliated by meandering into the roads. The market vendors did business with drivers who were stopped at intersections, adding to the confusion. While we waited for the light along with the jumble of honking cars and trucks that formed random lanes around us, I glanced out the window at the open-air shops. A sea of brightly clothed humanity appeared to be going everywhere and nowhere all at once. This river of colorful existence flowed into side alleys lined with booths, shops, and fruit stands that seemed to stretch on forever.

The traffic started up again, and we rumbled on in a cloud of exhaust until we stopped at another light. More waiting, more heat, more noise, more people flooding the streets. After half an hour of stopping, waiting, and driving again, we turned off the main road onto a quiet alley. The truck pitched along over the ruts until we turned the last corner and saw our administration center towering above rows of cars parked under slanting metal roofs. Swaying palms nestled the buildings and parking area.

This four-story building was the place our mission had its administration center and where missionaries gathered for workshops or came to do business and buy supplies. It was here that we were regularly refreshed by fellowship after months out in the village and where our children rejoined their friends for some fun and craziness. It had always been a bustling place, but not now.

I stepped out of the truck and thought how good it was to be back in a place so familiar that held so many happy memories! As we unpacked the truck, a few people came out to welcome us with hugs and exclamations of delight. They commented on how big our kids were, asked us about our trip, and ushered us inside. Yes, it was good to be back after our two-year furlough.

The next day, I went down into the yard to look around. As I walked the grounds, the old tree where the parrots had played now spread its branches so far that they nearly touched the neighboring apartments. There was the sandbox where my kids had fashioned cities in years gone by; now it was filled with weeds. I ambled by the sitting area under the carport where people had always gathered to chat, but now it was empty. I looked around with a growing odd feeling. Everything was technically the same and yet eerily different. In the yard, the swing set by the mango tree stood rusted with age and devoid of swings. As I stared at it in the empty silence, my mind brought back the happy clamor of missionary children swinging or climbing up the mango tree.

I went inside the building and looked at the closed doors of the ground floor offices that had always been the heart of the mission work of Wycliffe's Ivory Coast branch. These, too, were imbued with a somber quietness. I envisioned people coming in and out, talking in the hallways or congregating at the front door where the wooden carving of the forest antelope stood nursing her young. But the doors were closed now.

As I looked up the swirling steps of the winding central staircase, I remembered the children barreling up it, noisier than a troop of monkeys, to get their Cokes from the fridge up on the covered roof. The noise of the children and their images faded into the recesses of the past, and only the hollow emptiness of the building remained.

Walking soundlessly up those stairs, I reached the top floor, the scene of so many happy potlucks, coffee hours, and conference meetings. Looking at all the empty chairs by the tables, in my mind I filled the place once more with missionaries milling about, talking at tables, and gathering in groups. Children were horsing around as usual, the little ones running between the tables, and a few older ones throwing paper airplanes. Through the closed doors of the meeting hall, people enjoyed a meal together as the sun set behind the towering thunderheads that lined the evening sky. When the clouds faded from view in my mind, so did the people of the past. I was left again with silence in its place, apart from the soft breeze that played with the leaves of the potted plants that I had put there years before and the occasional bird flying by. I felt like something had died. In a way, it had—a way of life with a large extended "family" now scattered to the winds.

What had happened to turn this place into a near ghost town in such a short time? After we flew back to the States for a scheduled furlough in 2002, the Ivory Coast had experienced unrest so severe that the missionary families had left for safer grounds. Only a handful of missionaries had remained to keep the work going.[1]

A little background will help to understand what led to the unrest. When Ivory Coast gained its independence from France in 1960, Félix Houphouet-Boigny became president and held the post until his death in 1993. We came to Ivory Coast as a young family in 1988 and enjoyed the last few years of his presidency. He was a good president, and the country remained stable while he lived. After he died, his successor, Henri Konan Bédié was unable to carry on the legacy of stability. The country was plunged into chaos after a successful military coup in 1999 led by General Robert Guéï. Guéï promised to hold elections, and in October 2000 ran against opposition leader Laurent Gbagbo. Alassane Ouattara, another strong leader from the Muslim north, was also vying for power and would have been a formidable foe had he not been conveniently excluded by an electoral code that required both of a candidate's parents to be Ivorian nationals.

We had been in our village during that ill-fated election between Gbagbo and Guéï. As the results began to come in, and it became clear that Gbagbo was in the lead, the radio went dead. Hours later, the radio came back to life again

---

1. These events are detailed in my second book, *From the Village to the Ends of the Earth: Living and Working with a Bibleless People to Bring Them the Word of God* (Moscow, ID: Canon Press, 2020).

with the announcement that Guéï had won the election. The populace erupted into anger since they felt that the results had been rigged. They took to the streets in protest, and Guéï had to flee. Gbagbo was proclaimed president, but the situation remained unstable. Ouattara's supporters felt that he should not have been banned from running, and Ouattara called for a new election.

Pockets of fighting broke out between Ouattara's supporters in the north and Gbagbo's supporters in the south. In 2001, there was a failed coup attempt on Gbagbo. After this, the two leaders met and tried to iron out their differences and reach an agreement to prevent further violence.

But the turmoil continued, and our planned six-month furlough turned into two years after another coup attempt against Gbagbo in September 2002. Guéï was blamed for the coup and was subsequently killed, while Ouattara fled to the French embassy. Eventually, it became known that a new rebel group called the New Forces had carried out the coup, and this group also fled back to the north. The growing conflict was now shifting into one between the north and the south. Bouaké, Ivory Coast's second largest city, situated in the middle of the country, acted as a buffer zone between the rival factions. The United Nations came to keep this zone stable and prevent the country from going to war.

Things began to look hopeful when Gbagbo accepted a peace deal that created a power-sharing government with the northern opposition. In May 2003, a ceasefire was signed with the rebels. At a ceremony in July, the military chiefs and rebels declared that the war was over. We were thrilled and hoped we could return to the Ivory Coast that year, but it ended up an uneasy truce, and our administration center remained mostly deserted.

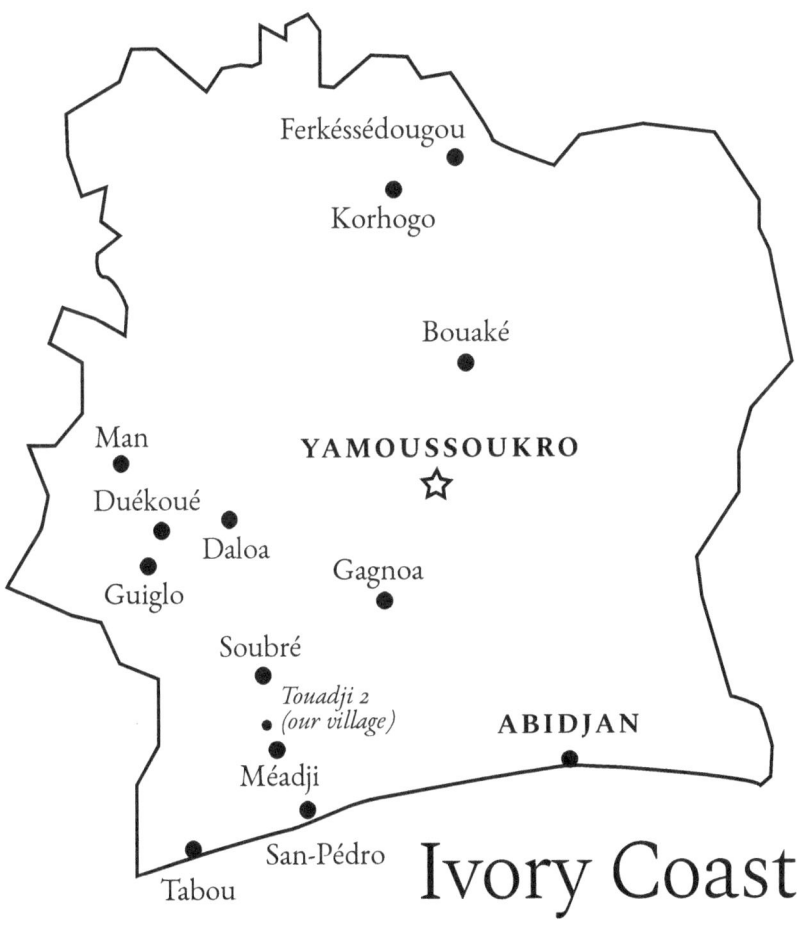

Chapter 2

Preparing for Our Return

> These things I have spoken to you, that in Me you may have peace. In the world you will have tribulation; but be of good cheer, I have overcome the world. (John 16:33)

IN MARCH 2004, DEADLY CLASHES OCcurred in the capital city of Abidjan at a rally in opposition to the president. All summer, we prayed about whether we should return. We asked God to guide us because, in addition to the country's instability, my health was also worrisome. We sought the Lord on both issues, looking to Him for answers. Csaba called colleagues who were still in Ivory

Coast to find out the latest news. One missionary said, "Things are calm for now, with possible trouble on the horizon. But this has happened before, and we may end up being in this holding state for another ten years."

We didn't want the Bible translation to be on hold for ten years while we *wondered* if something might happen. What we wanted to know, which was impossible without divine eyes, was whether the country would reach a point of tempest where our lives could be in danger. The uncertainty caused us to constantly look up to God for answers.

Meanwhile, there was the question of whether I could physically handle going back. Something was not right with my health, and I maintained an unsteady truce with my body. If I was nice to it, then everything was nearly tolerable. I had to be very careful with how I spent my limited energy. If I overdid it in the least, I would end up in bed for days trying to recover.

We went to specialists who did numerous tests and found nothing wrong with me except what they simply called *chronic fatigue* for want of a better explanation. According to the lab results, I was even healthier than I had been before the fatigue began. Things were not right, though. I had all the members of the orchestra, but they just couldn't play together.

We discussed what it would mean for me to go back to Africa. I didn't want to even consider staying in the States due to my fatigue, but we questioned whether there might be some serious underlying cause. In the meantime, we traveled from Idaho to Illinois in May 2004 to visit my parents and rest up before, we hoped, leaving for Ivory Coast. After some weeks, my energy did pull up a little. But why had the flight from Idaho taken such a severe toll on me? It put me in bed for days, and that was just traveling across the country. Could I even handle *traveling* to Ivory Coast, let alone living there?

After analyzing the situation, we decided to return to the village in stages, stopping along the way so I could recover at each point. We'd go to Abidjan and stay at the administration center until I pulled up. Then we would travel the six hours to the missionary guesthouse in San Pédro by the ocean and rest a couple more days. After that, we would undertake the two-hour drive to our village, Touadji 2. If I could only get to the village, I would have Janvier, our cook, to help with the housework. It was potentially doable, and if God kept the door open even a crack, we wanted to go through it.

In the meantime, we waited at my parents' house in Illinois for the situation in Ivory Coast to clear up and the administration in Abidjan to give us the go-ahead to come back. As usual, the children kept busy. Andreas and Noai played their Irish whistles in Grandma's big maple tree like a treetop band of Celtic fairies. Andreas and Jeremiah took to harassing the squirrels in the backyard with their toy pellet guns, which transformed the squirrels into nervous, hyper individuals with filthy mouths. Jeremiah also liked carving wood. In fact, he didn't stop at wood but went on to carve his hand as well, which landed him in the emergency room for the fourth time in his life.

One day, two salesmen came to my parents' door. Both looked African, but only one was. Csaba told them that he didn't want to buy any magazine subscriptions since we were heading back to Africa. The African perked up and asked, "What part of Africa?"

Csaba responded, "Ivory Coast."

"That's where I'm from!" he exclaimed excitedly.

The man said he was a Beté, which is a people group that borders the Bakwé, so Csaba greeted him in his native tongue. The man danced for joy and then started talking to Csaba in Ivorian French.

The American got agitated. "What is he saying to you, man? Tell me what he is saying. I can't understand him!"

The African responded, "He's speaking my language! He's speaking my language! It's so sweet. What they're doing is really good!"

Your mother tongue has the power to speak to your heart in a way that no other language can. That is why we are translating the Bible into Bakwé.

LEAVING FOR IVORY COAST

As we followed the situation in Ivory Coast, we learned that there had been talks about the country disarming

PREPARING FOR OUR RETURN

completely. Csaba heard that some missionaries were even returning. We got the green light from our administration to leave for Africa in October 2004. It would be different this time since we were only given permission to visit our village for three months before heading north to the calmer country of Mali to resume our work. Most of Wycliffe's Ivory Coast branch, including our director, Robert, had relocated there due to the unrest. We also would be returning with only three of our four children since Hans would be staying in the States for college. The others would be doing homeschool. Our daughter Noai would be a senior, Andreas a freshman, and Jeremiah still in grade school.

And so, after that stormy flight over the Sahara, we had arrived at the administration center in Abidjan. We were back in Ivory Coast, but we still had to determine whether it was safe to return to the village or if we would need to remain in the capital city.

Csaba talked with other missionaries and some of our African coworkers about the political situation. One of the missionaries wrote back, "Here in town, things are very calm. Abidjan has had a few demonstrations, but things have not exploded, and who knows how long we will keep going between war and peace. Lots of talk, but nothing concrete happens . . . . I would not be surprised to spend the next few years listening to this rhetoric until either Ivory Coast runs out of money or someone changes the government." We were encouraged by this and by the news that the missionary boarding school in Bouaké was running again with twenty-five students. We prayed that when and if change came, it would come in a peaceful way.

Our Bakwé coworkers, Alexis, Firmain, and Perez, came down to Abidjan from the village to do their yearly planning and evaluation of the translation project with Csaba. When Csaba asked about the safety of the roads, they said the main roads seemed clear of highway robbers, but it was still hard for the average person to travel, because every time the bus stopped at checkpoints, they had to pay 2,000 CFA[1] in bribes (about five U.S. dollars) due to identity card issues. Evidently, during the last president's administration, some government officials had been issuing false identity cards. To add to the confusion, hooligans had burned some of the government offices that held birth certificate records. Since you needed a birth certificate to get a new identity card, getting identification papers became a nightmarish experience of red tape and fees and officials absent from their desks during work hours. The best solution was to just pay a lot of money in bribes.

While Csaba was busy with the Bakwé team, I was preoccupied with preparations for the village. I happened to glance out the window one day during this work and saw Andreas on his way to the crown of a five-story coconut palm. He was already high up when I spotted him. Startled,

---

1. Communauté Financière Africaine (Central African Community) francs, a currency used by several Central African countries.

I called to him to come back down. Even though that didn't appeal to him, he obeyed and descended. To get into the crown of a palm tree, you must flip upside down and then pull yourself up by the palm fronds. If you miscalculate or if there is a loose frond, you'll fall straight down five stories and land on your head!

As we prepared to leave for the village, it troubled me that my strength hadn't returned, even after several days of rest. I asked, "Lord, what are you doing?" But hadn't we been in difficult situations before, and hadn't God gotten us through? If God was faithful then, He would be faithful now.

One incident of answered prayer from the past had always encouraged me in times like this. At the beginning of our schooling with Wycliffe, we had very little money. One day, I told Csaba that we only had enough food to last for a few more days, and we still needed to pay the monthly school bill. Csaba had recently gotten a part-time job to help with expenses, but he wouldn't get paid for another two weeks. So we prayed.

And God quickly answered. I found a box of fruit with a *free* sign on it at the dorms. Later, someone gave me some frozen meat unexpectedly. Then, when we went to talk with the bursar about our schooling bill, we found that it had already been paid by an anonymous giver.

We still needed more food, and we had only five dollars left to buy what we needed for the two weeks until

Csaba was paid. While I was in line at the store with my two bags of dried rice and beans (all we had money for), a stranger tapped me on the shoulder and said, "This may seem strange, but God is telling me to give you this money." I thanked her, got out of line, and got the rest of what we needed. It was just enough to last until Csaba got paid. That episode encouraged us that God would be watching out for us in the future, too.

Chapter 3

What a Night!

IT IS NOT AN ABSENCE OF TROUBLE THAT brings peace, but a resting of the mind on Christ.

We headed out to the village on Tuesday with a planned stop for a few days at the Christian and Missionary Alliance (CMA) guesthouse on the coast in San-Pédro. After a six-hour drive, we turned down the beachfront road and saw the familiar string of restaurants topped by a forest of coconut trees. Beyond that was the ocean, its waves sweeping across the glistening shore, lit up by the sun. It beckoned to us, but we had to leave that glory for the moment and head to the guesthouse.

We were greeted by Julie B. (who helped run the guesthouse with her husband Greg) and her teenage daughter

Theresa. Julie said that Greg was gone but would return soon. After unloading our things in the upper-floor apartment, we grabbed our towels and drove down to the beach. It felt so good to have the salty wind in our faces, the sand squeaking under our feet, and the waves beating on the shore in that intoxicating way. The ocean seemed like a living creature catching the light of the sun and scattering it into a thousand sparkling gems upon its surface.

My kids ran down the sloping beach and jumped into the foaming water. I lay down on a towel wishing I could swim, too, but I had no more energy left. Something felt really wrong, and after half an hour, I told Csaba I needed to go back to the apartment to lie down. I was sinking fast.

The next day Csaba wrote an update to our extended family:

> Dear Family,
>
> We heard that the south attacked the rebels at Bouaké this morning by air and are trying to liberate the north by force. We are in San-Pédro, and everything was calm today. We got a call from our director in Mali telling us that Bouaké was under attack and to stay here a bit longer to find out if the fighting would spread. Then we received a call from the American Embassy checking in on us.
>
> I went into town to stock up on provisions just in case the stores closed down. I bought a 50-lb. bag

each of flour, sugar, and powdered milk, as well as canned goods and some frozen meat. Greg was up in the rebel-held north reclaiming his truck and arrived this evening. He had a lot of stories to tell. Apparently, the north's economy is booming and has never been better. Produce and merchandise are coming in from the north untaxed and un-hassled, so they are not sure they want to be delivered.

We will be listening to the news and trying to make a decision on what to do. If it comes to evacuation, we would rather be in San-Pédro and get evacuated with the other Americans. However, if the fighting stays in the north, then we could go on to the village. We will have to ask advice from our leadership in Mali as well as the American Embassy first.

We thank the Lord for how smoothly we were able to return and make the trip to San-Pédro. We know that He is in control and that He will watch over us.

Grace and peace in Christ,
Csaba

Around nightfall on Wednesday, an African friend of Greg and Julie came from town with the news that a crowd was burning down the French school. The government forces had decided to break the yearlong peace treaty by bombing Bouaké in preparation for retaking it. This wouldn't have affected us except that they inadvertently (they claimed) bombed French forces in a peace-keeping barracks, killing nine soldiers. Within minutes, the French had retaliated by destroying the entire Ivorian fleet of a few grounded military aircraft. This act of French aggression changed the focus of the conflict from the rebel north toward the French, resulting in French-owned businesses being looted and French citizens being attacked. In San-Pédro, the mob was on the rampage and apparently had plans to head to the beachfront corridor to destroy anything French. The problem was that the CMA guesthouse was right in their path, and we looked awfully French with our light-colored skin!

Csaba turned on the radio and heard that all four French schools in Abidjan had been burned and whites were being dragged out of cars and beaten, some seriously hurt, and others even killed. The mobs had tried to take the airport but were repelled by French forces. Commercial airlines were forced to cancel their flights, and the American embassy told Americans to stay inside because of the unrest. We were warned that a large group was on the streets of San-Pédro unleashing their anger.

We took action immediately and made preparations for fleeing if the guesthouse was attacked. If the mob arrived at our place, we planned to disappear into the thick forest behind the guesthouse, where we would stay hidden until danger passed. We packed two small backpacks with necessary items in case we had to spend the night in the forest. I wanted to pack my large Bible, but it was too heavy, so we put in a small Gideon Bible that my dad, a Gideon, had given us, plus flashlights, batteries, water, food, some plastic to sit on, insect repellent, a small container of medicines, and a malaria treatment. The kids put in only the essentials of toothbrushes, travel Bibles, and their Irish whistles. If pursued, we would make our way deep into the rainforest, trying to elude our pursuers until we could make it out safely on the other side. We didn't know what would happen from there, but at this point we didn't have many options.

Besides us, only Greg, Julie, and Theresa were at the guesthouse. Greg told us to put on dark pants and shoes to protect against snakes and mosquitoes and to make our flight less noticeable. This was problematic since I hadn't brought any pants to Africa. Csaba unearthed a pair that I had saved for Europe, and I borrowed a pair of shoes.

Even before we finished packing, I was exhausted to the point where I couldn't stand for long. I had a sinking, weak feeling like the earth was dropping out and me with it. I called on God to give me strength, because I didn't know how I was going to get through the night if we had to flee.

The men gave us a machete and one of the walkie talkies. Csaba told us to go to an apartment in the far back of the compound. We were to stay out of sight while he and Greg guarded the front gate with the night guardsman. The plan was that if they heard anyone coming, they would radio for us to slip out the back and hide in the rainforest until they joined us.

The kids and I went to bed around 11 p.m. with our clothes and shoes on. I tried to sleep but tossed and turned until 12:30 a.m. when I drifted off into a fitful sleep only to be woken by three distant gun shots and Greg radioing us to get out. I went in and woke the kids. The girls, the dog, and the parrot were up in a flash, and so was Andreas, who had been on the couch, but it took a while for Jeremiah to wake. As Julie and I headed for the door, we noticed that our troops were all lined up at the bathroom. We urged them to follow us immediately, and we left the apartment.

Once out the iron door in the back of the compound, we faced a thick wall of solid green, the gateway to the rainforest beyond. I searched the tangled wall with my flashlight and found a small tunnel on the right. We slipped into it and went down a dark path with a low ceiling that wound into the hidden depths of the forest. We went on cautiously, shining the light ahead so that we wouldn't stumble on a cobra, since they liked to come out at night. We didn't want to go too far without the men, or they wouldn't be able to find us. After a bit, we found a wider section of the path and sat down on our plastic.

Turning off our flashlights, we waited there in the dead of night, surrounded by all the sounds that a tropical rain forest can make. We were well hidden, but not exactly quiet. The puppy was nervous and had to be hushed, and the parrot felt insecure and kept whistling a concerned "What's up?" into the darkness.

After a long twenty minutes, we got radio contact from the men that all was still quiet at the front gate. Evidently, the gunshots had been farther out than they had thought. Some other missionaries in town had called and told them that a large mob had come to their front gate, but their guard insisted that they were American, not French, and demanded that the mob leave them alone. The mob smashed their water meter but left without doing further harm.

There we sat in the darkness, knowing we could be next. The dog finally hushed, but the parrot continued to whistle his anxieties into the night. We couldn't see out of the forest, but I could hear distant gunshots. Finally, I saw Csaba's flashlight bobbing around the corner of the path, and he told us it was safe to come back for now since the gunfire didn't seem close. We picked up our plastic and followed him back to the apartment.

Once we were safely inside, Csaba and Greg went back to the front gate. Both were armed, Csaba with a machete and Greg with a double-headed ax. Csaba's idea was to stick to the original plan of staying on the inside of the iron gate, which would allow them time to sound the alarm for us to get out and for them to then follow. Greg offered to station himself outside of the gate to take on the mob with his ax, but both the night guardsman and Csaba pleaded with him to stay on the inside. He came in, and they locked the door. The wall was low enough to be scaled, but it would at least buy them time to get us out. They sat down with their weapons and listened to the gunfire coming from town.

As we lay in the back apartment, we could hear the gunfire as well, and it made me wonder what the mobs were doing to the French and what they would do to us if they got drunk enough. At 2:00 a.m., Julie and I heard cannon fire in the distance, so I radioed to Csaba to ask what was going on. Csaba came back and told us that the French were probably being attacked at the airport.

I went outside to talk more to him and express my concerns about our predicament. What would we do? How would we get out? I knew African history of how awful one group could be to another when in a rage. Csaba said we could only trust the Lord and wait for the next step to unfold. Noai came out and talked, too, since she couldn't sleep.

Csaba left for the front again, while I stayed up since I was too restless to sleep. As I pondered our precarious situation, I was uneasy. I looked up at the night sky. The stars shone so brilliant against the dark expanse. The entire firmament seemed grand and peaceful, even in the midst of this chaos below. I wished I was up there in that peace and out of the imminent danger. The heavens didn't seem like they had a care in the world. Yet all that grandeur was God's way of reminding me that *He* didn't have a care in the world, because He was in complete control. If He had peace, why shouldn't I? His was a higher peace that couldn't be touched by trouble, a peace vividly highlighted by the darkness around us.

I relaxed and went back to bed around 3:00 am. I was totally exhausted and feeling much worse, but now I was at peace. I also knew that Csaba and Greg would be there all night guarding that gate. I thought to myself, "My, what men they are! Willing to put themselves between us and a gang of drunk, gun-toting marauders, armed with only a machete and a double-headed ax!"

The next morning, things were calm, and Greg went into town to see what damage had been done. Many of the French businesses had been ransacked and burned, and looting was still ongoing. A large store that sold house and yard equipment was gutted. They were even removing the roofing! Greg told us that the Sophia, a luxury hotel on the beach, had windows smashed and items taken. Another hotel that was only five hundred meters from the guesthouse had been heavily looted as well. Evidently, the pickings at the hotels were good, and the looters had found the liquor stash and become too drunk to continue looting. We were told by our informant that the mob would return tonight to finish the job of attacking the French houses along the beachfront corridor. Over the radio, the president told everyone to calm down and quit looting and destroying, but it didn't look like anyone was going to listen.

Csaba napped that afternoon in case he had to be on watch again through the night. The rest of us, who had at least slept a little during the night, started filling every possible container with water since the power and water were often cut in times of unrest. Thankfully, Csaba and Greg had stocked up on rice, milk, and flour. When we had finished the preparations, Julie and I rested while the kids played games.

We found out later that the night's rage toward the French had been planned, and there had been attacks in other major cities throughout the country as well. But it was not over yet.

Chapter 4

Evacuation

> Lay all your loads and your weights by faith upon Christ. Ease yourself and let Him bear all. He can, He does, He will bear you. (Samuel Rutherford, *The Loveliness of Christ*)

WE KNEW THE MOB'S NEW ANGER TOward the French could be extremely vicious. This put us in grave danger since we could easily be mistaken for French, and no one was likely to ask for our passports to check. We were also concerned about the possibility of the mob's focus shifting from the initial target of French citizens to the wider group of all foreigners. The president made another speech to the nation, calling on everyone to settle down, return to their houses, and stop attacking the French.

We prayed and asked God for wisdom regarding whether we should continue as planned to the village and hunker down there or try to leave the country. We were too familiar with what had happened to whites in other countries not to know what could happen to us now if we stayed. The embassies were offering voluntary evacuations for those wanting to get out. The Kings, an older missionary couple with Baptist Mid-Missions acting as our embassy contact, asked if we wanted to be evacuated. After talking with our director, Robert Hale, we decided to wait where we were and see what happened. If things settled down, the best scenario would be for us to go on to the village where people knew us. There would be some level of protection there.

Thursday night was fast approaching. Greg's African informant gave us intel that the mob was planning to attack the two French houses near us. Csaba and Greg warned the neighbors. Soon after, an armed military guard arrived to spend the night on our street. They said they would protect the guesthouse as well. Since the military was outside, we stayed in our own apartment rather than the back apartment where we'd retreated the previous night, but we still didn't know what to expect. Csaba wanted to stay up, but by midnight he was so exhausted that he fell fast sleep. Even though we slept, we were not relaxed, and when a car horn sounded in the middle of the night, both Csaba and I shot out of bed so quickly that I almost passed out. Csaba went to the window to see if we needed to slip out the back again, but it was only a changing of the military guard.

On Friday morning, Csaba and Greg went out to buy more supplies. On the way, they saw two large businesses that had been gutted and ransacked by the mobs. Apart from that, people were back on the streets and things were looking more normal. They drove past the Assemblies of God guesthouse, which was run by a French missionary, and saw it had been looted. There was a stove and some other litter in the yard, and the gates were lying on the ground. They wondered about the missionary. We later heard that she had been in her house when she heard the mob coming and had slipped out back to hide in the forest. While she was hiding, the gang trashed her place and took most of her belongings. They even came back a second time a day or two later and took items like doors and mirrors that they had missed before. Before she left the country, an African man showed up at her door with her stolen microwave and asked her how to use it. She retorted, "You put your hand in it and turn it on."

Back at the guesthouse, Csaba printed up American flags to put on our truck. He knew that the Bakwé words which were written all over the truck would also help. I made sure the water jugs were filled in case the water went out again.

We hoped that the worst was over since the town seemed to be returning to normal. Csaba called Alexis to find out what the conditions were on the road to the village. Alexis told him it was still blocked and that we should wait. On the radio, the French, Ivorian, and UN generals tried to calm everyone down by showing the populace that they were unified. The French general told everyone that France had no intention of taking over the country and overthrowing the president, which was the current rumor. He reassured the people that the French were friends with Ivory Coast, not enemies. The Ivorian general ordered everyone to stop the rumors and quit attacking French properties. He then told them to get off the streets, quit looting, clean up the trash, and get back to work.

Robert told us that the crisis management team was not thinking of evacuating us anymore, and it would be better to leave Ivory Coast for Mali in January as we had planned. However, he added that if all the other missionaries were going to leave, we should evacuate with them to avoid being in the region without support. The kids strongly pleaded for us to stay even if all the French left, but Csaba told them to pack only a few things in an evacuation bag in case we had to fly out. The rest of that day, I did homeschooling, and in the afternoon we went to the beach. No one else was there except a few workers cleaning up the broken glass and chairs. We also passed a military guard with guns.

I lay down on a towel on the sand because I was again too tired to swim. I looked at the water and longed to be in it. The kids had fun in the ocean, and it was so good for them to relax after the tension. When we returned home, we got word from the Baptists that they were all thinking of pulling out, which meant there would be no more missionaries left in the area except for Greg and Julie. We asked why they were leaving, and they said that a Christian Ivorian friend who worked high up had urged them to get out as fast as possible because, from her vantage point, it seemed like the worst of the danger was yet to come—what we were experiencing was just the swell of turbulent waters ahead of the tidal wave. We got a call from the Kings telling us that the French had another evacuation plane ready and that we needed to sign up before 11 a.m. the next morning if we wanted to leave on it. We didn't sign up because Csaba hadn't talked with our director about this new bit of information yet.

We weren't sure what to think about this turn of events. We discussed the risks, still wondering if the crisis would blow over and what would be best for me in my weakened state. Csaba knew what could happen when a populace went into a rage. He remembered a time when one ethnic group had turned on another and killed two hundred people, and it hadn't even made the Ivorian news. We had only learned of the situation because the refugees came into our area.

We had never felt directly threatened before, but we wondered whether things had changed now. If we had to stay, we would be safest waiting it out in the village, and I would have a chance to recover there. But if the country seriously blew up, the escape routes could be blocked. We also questioned what message it would send to the people in the village if we left. On the other hand, if things became really dangerous, how could Csaba knowingly lead his family into a hemmed-in and potentially deadly situation? These considerations all weighed heavily on our minds, but Csaba was looking in faith to God for wisdom to make the right decision.

Just after we received this new information from the Baptists, Robert called again and told us the leadership was ordering us to head north to Mali immediately. They were alarmed by the hate speeches against all foreigners airing on the radio. One of the Baptist missionaries shared that they had been through the Congo rebellion and that there were many similarities in the current climate to the one in the Congo before it blew up. We also received a call from our home church's missions deacon who told us that the elders were feeling very uneasy and wanted us out. He said we should not hesitate to leave our stuff behind and go. We appreciated their oversight and direction that made our course of action clear.

As we made plans that evening for leaving San-Pédro, we asked Robert for permission to go by road rather than by evacuation plane since we wanted to take our books and clothes with us on a commercial flight the following Wednesday. The evacuation flights were only allowing one small carry-on per passenger. Robert felt uneasy about the land route because if gangs riled up by the hate speeches were blocking the roads, our truck could be ambushed. He told us we could only go if we found out it was safe enough.

 Csaba called the village and asked Alexis to ask an informant from the bus lines if the roads to Abidjan were safe. Alexis reported that there were no mobs on the roads and that everything appeared normal. Greg and Julie were planning to leave at 5:00 the next morning, and they offered to convoy together. Csaba called Abidjan and arranged for us to fly out from there on Wednesday.

 There was still some question if Wednesday would be too late to get out safely. Csaba called the American Embassy to find out, and the vice-consul told him that she felt this was the eye of the storm and that we might have only a small window to get out before the worst hit. The United Nations was going to vote on putting sanctions on the Ivory Coast. Once the sanctions were announced on Monday, the rage could shift toward Americans.

 Alexis came that night to take our extra things back to the village in the morning. Harry and Reidun Groots, Dutch missionary friends serving with New Tribes Mission, also drove to the guesthouse in preparation for evacuating. When they arrived, they looked extremely weary. They told us that after they evacuated, they would not be coming back. That is one of the hardest things about missionary life; one moment you have close friends, and the next you might never see them again. But for the time being, we enjoyed what fellowship we could. Our children played Irish music, and everyone relaxed as they listened. Later, Noai cooked dinner for us all.

By then, I was feeling horrible. I told Csaba that I didn't know if I had the energy to do this. He reassured me that God would help. We headed out on Saturday morning at five o'clock, before the sun was up. As we drove away in the dark, we noticed a group of young men on the road who eyed us suspiciously and called us to pull over. We ignored them and kept going, but they approached, and one of them slapped our truck as we passed. We wondered if they would make trouble, but the gang left us unscathed. The next precarious place would be the police checkpoint at the intersection heading to Abidjan, where they could harass us and refuse our departure.

When we came to the intersection, there was a lineup of cars, mostly foreigners wanting to flee. We were told that the guards would not open the barrier until 6 a.m., when it got light. An uneasy restlessness was in the air as the cars sat silently. Csaba went to talk to the guards to determine whether the atmosphere was hostile. He found a Bakwé guard who had heard of him. Csaba switched to talking in Bakwé, which formed an immediate bond. When the sun came up, we were waved on. As we turned at the intersection, I looked down the road that led to our village and felt like my heart was being wrenched in two as we headed the other direction. I didn't know when I would ever see the village, the people, our house, or our pets again. Yet God knew exactly what He was doing, and I knew it was for good. He was asking us to trust Him and to come along quietly in the process. We hoped that He would bring us back to Ivory Coast again.

Traveling on the coastal road wasn't as dangerous as predicted, and we entered Abidjan no worse for wear. Back at the administration center, we were met by the Abidjan staff who had been so concerned for us. They knew we had arrived when they heard the welcome sound of the kids playing their whistles outside. No matter what difficult times we were experiencing, our kids played music through it all, bringing comfort to many a troubled heart.

Our Abidjan colleagues told us that the day we arrived was the first day they had ventured out of the administration center. They, too, had heard gunfire on the night of the looting and had seen apartments and houses ransacked across the way. A group of young men had tried to enter our center but were turned back by neighbors vouching for us. As looting went on nearby, they saw helicopters flying in to evacuate the French.

That day, Abidjan was calm. God had given us a window of relative peace to travel in, and we were grateful. The airport had been closed just days before because it had been targeted by the rioters. Then the French took control of the airport so that they could get their own people out. The radio announced that more than 7,000 French citizens had left Ivory Coast. We later learned that over 1,000 missionaries had already left. Missionaries are often the last ones out when a country is in turmoil.

We called Sam Watkins, an American friend from the Baptist group back in San-Pédro, and told him the road was clear. His group had decided to drive to Abidjan the morning after us because the French hadn't come through with the evacuation plane they had planned to take from San-Pédro. The Groots had already left on another plane, and the Kings were waiting for a second promised evacuation plane because they were afraid for the safety of their French helper on the roads.

The question of whether to leave the country sooner than Wednesday remained. If we misjudged and were trapped in the city during a civil war, it was likely that food, water, electricity, and medical help would become scarce. Csaba weighed the variables. The Italians were providing an evacuation plane at 6 p.m. Sunday on a first-come, first-served basis, with Italians having priority. If we were able to get on this flight, we would have to leave most of our stuff. However, I was already extremely weak; if we took the risk and stayed, then something happened, it could be disastrous. We only had a short window of time to decide, so we prayed, asking God what to do.

On Saturday night, as we were still pondering these things, we heard an angry mob yelling below our apartment. Noai ran to the window to see what was going on, but Csaba ordered her back. Csaba turned on the radio and heard that the government had cut all power to the north, angering the rebels further. They were planning to march on the south and attack. We were in the target city, and there was no more forest to run to. We couldn't even drive out now because the borders would be shut down. Alexis called Csaba from the village to express his concern. "Now we're in for it. You've got to leave now. We'll have no peace until you are out safely."

We got word from the U.S. embassy that trouble was brewing and we were to get out of the country any way we could. By this time, even the kids were beginning to feel overloaded on war talk and decided to play a game as a distraction. No one even wanted to hear the latest developments. We prepared to leave Sunday on the Italian evacuation plane.

That night, we packed our carry-on bags and told the kids that we could lose everything we left behind if the center was taken. They put in what meant most to them: their instruments and Gideon Bibles. Noai added her art stuff, and Jeremiah included a carved boat that he and his dad were making together. Noai suggested that she didn't need a change of clothes so that she could put in more valuable things like her violin. I insisted that she needed some clothing, and after a little discussion, she complied. The violin stayed.

After Csaba put the laptop in his bag along with his other work equipment, I noticed that he had forgotten to put in any clothes. He told me he didn't need any and would rather add more books. I suggested that he did need a change of something, and he put in a few items. I packed what I could but had to leave all the schoolbooks, games, reading material, most of the vitamins and medicines we had stocked up on for the next two years, the carving tools, Noai's violin, the cookbooks, and the Christmas presents.

Greg, Julie, and Theresa arrived on Sunday morning. As Greg came in, he smiled and said, "You just can't get rid of us, can you?" They were fun to be with, and our shared joking, teasing, and music eased the tension. Noai cooked us lunch with what she could find around the place. We ate white beans garnished with hotdogs and a side dish of carrots and peas with more white beans. I asked why she didn't make a dessert with white beans, and she just smiled. The meal fueled a lot more teasing about the effect it would have, and we ate our beans in good humor. Afterwards, we headed for the airport five hours before the departure time to make sure we got a spot on the plane. Ambroise, the manager of the Abidjan administration center, drove us via a back route to avoid dangerous spots where gangs were still on the roads.

As we went through town, the damage from the past week was evident. French businesses were burned, litter and broken glass covered the streets, and the skeletons of burned-out taxi cabs dotted the roadsides, monuments to the ongoing conflict. Closer to the airport, we passed army trucks, rolls of barbed wire, and military tanks. It felt like we were passing through a war zone, and, in a way, we were. The airport glass had huge cracks and bullet holes from the nights of looting. After the French military allowed us inside, we registered with the Italian officials and sat down on an empty luggage conveyor belt. The place was almost devoid of civilians.

I was tired and weak but tried not to think about it. I still had a plane flight to go before I could collapse. Andreas and Noai played Celtic music on their whistles. The airport reverberated with the song and turned a war zone into a party. Then the other conveyor belt started up. I had always wanted to ride one, so Julie and I got on. We jumped off right before it went behind the wall, but our kids kept going and rode the full route.

Sam's family finally arrived from San-Pédro with the other Baptist missionaries. They had come by road after we gave them the all clear. We also found out that this would be the last evacuation flight. The Kings had hurriedly left San-Pédro by road after their French evacuation flight fell through like Sam's had before, and we prayed for them to arrive in time to make the Italian flight. I lay on the stationary conveyor belt, too weak to sit up. As the 6 p.m. flight time approached, a crew of Korean diplomats arrived along with more Italians. We were told that seating was limited, but since we had come early, we were still on. The other missionary families wondered what would happen to them, but, in the end, they made it on, too.

The Kings arrived at the airport just before the plane was scheduled to leave (the departure had been put off an hour) and were told there was no more room. After pleading, they were somehow able to get on the flight. As we waited, someone got a phone call and learned that the U.S. embassy had bumped its danger status to the highest alert.

Around 7 p.m., we checked our bags and were escorted out onto the tarmac. As we walked into the night past French troops, I noticed that all the commercial airplanes were missing. We walked on toward a C-130 military transport plane with a belly like a whale.

The belly opened, a ramp was lowered, and we climbed into what looked like a boiler room with tubes, ladders, and hooks for parachutes on the walls. All hopes of complimentary drinks and peanuts disappeared! Our seats were nets lowered from the ceiling facing each other. The seat belts were too large, so we slid around when the plane took off, but the kids didn't care—this was way too much fun.

The engines roared as the plane went down the runway, and we had to yell to hear one another. Steam poured from huge pipes to pressurize the compartment. Once we were safely in the air, the crew turned off the lights. As the plane hummed, vibrated, and shook in flight, I looked out the tiny window high above us and saw lightning flashing outside. Somehow, it seemed to represent the other kind of storm we had just been through.

After an hour-long flight, we touched down in Accra, Ghana. Here were the commercial planes! Rows of Air Ivoire jets were all moored on the side of the tarmac here in Ghana where they would be safe. We were escorted off the evacuation plane and stood in long lines waiting to be classed as refugees by the American embassy. I was fading so badly that I sat down on anything that would hold me as we inched forward in the queue. We finally made it to the head of the line, where a lady from the American embassy told us we needed to go back to the beginning of the line and fill out a visa form for our stay in Ghana. After turning around, filling out papers, and waiting for two more hours, we were finally free to leave for the Wycliffe guesthouse in Accra where Robert had made reservations for us.

We felt relieved to be out of the pressure cooker of Ivory Coast and in the milder stew of Ghana. We still had the inconveniences of traveling in West Africa in front of us. Getting to Mali would not be easy—but at least we were out

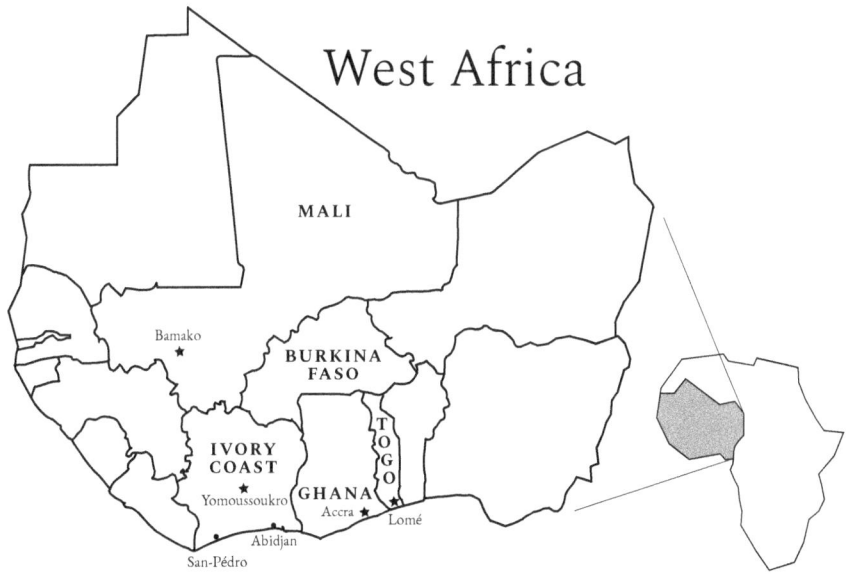

of danger. We arrived at the guesthouse dead tired and were welcomed by two older Wycliffe missionaries. They were sympathetic and did everything to make our stay comfortable. When our kids played their Irish whistles, it delighted everyone. I was impressed with how the kids had handled this dangerous affair. They were helpful and cheerful and hadn't crumbled in fear. We were proud of them.

Chapter 5

There and Back Again

> If I come to heaven any way, howbeit like a tired traveler upon my Guide's shoulder, it is good enough for those who have no legs of their own for such a journey. I never thought there had been so much wrestling to win to the top of that steep mountain as now I find. (Samuel Rutherford)

THE NEXT DAY, AFTER MOST OF US HAD slept well, Greg and Csaba returned to the airport to get tickets to Mali. To their dismay, they found that there were no direct flights. This was highly disappointing, but Csaba learned that we could fly to Mali from Togo instead, which was the next country over. The flight from Accra to Lomé, the capital of Togo, was in a week's time, which seemed too long. The only other option was to take a three-hour trip to the border by road and go on to the airport by another taxi.

Csaba and Greg found some taxis willing to take us to the border. Csaba called the American embassy and asked if we could get visas at the border since the Togo embassy was closed for a holiday. They didn't know if we could or not but thought it possible. When Robert called, Csaba told him the situation. Robert bought our plane tickets and arranged for Jim Green, an American Wycliffe missionary in Lomé, to meet us at the airport and give us our tickets. It was wonderful that Wycliffe operated in so many countries.

In the meantime, we had no way of contacting the outside world. All that our son Hans knew was that we were in danger and trying to get out of the country. We asked Robert to email Hans to keep him updated.

After a day of rest, I was thankful that I was just strong enough to travel. At 6 a.m., we drove off from the Accra guesthouse in two taxis. As we rode, I looked out the window and saw the lazy calm of Ghana passing by. It felt so refreshing not to feel like a hunted animal.

Near the border, we entered a crowded city with narrow streets and a jumble of vehicles. For ten minutes, we lost sight of the other taxi with our kids in it, but on a back road we met up again and continued to a parking lot outside the customs building. While the men paid the taxi drivers and arranged for them to carry our luggage over the border on foot, we waited in the hot tropical sun, feeling a bit like fried eggs. We then walked toward a growing throng of people entering the Ghana customs building. We passed one inspection after another and finally ended up on the other side at Togo's customs office. The men went inside the building, where it took them a full hour to fill out visa forms, which thankfully were being issued that day. The official said that there had been a steady stream of refugees coming out of Ivory Coast and was very sympathetic.

While the men were in the Togo customs building, the rest of us stayed outside leaning against a wall, mostly in the sun. We could see the ocean on the other side of the market but felt little breeze. Sweat dripped down our backs. After a while, Csaba arranged for me to sit inside because by now I could barely stand. As time wore on, some of the kids began to feel faint as well.

Finally, when all the paperwork was done, Csaba and Greg arranged for a couple of taxis to take us to the airport for our 2:00 p.m. flight to Mali. We were met by Jim Green, who handed us our tickets. Robert had arranged it all again! We knew Jim was busy, so we told him he didn't have to stay. He laughed and said, "I'm going to stay *right here* until I see that plane with my own eyes, and you on it."

Csaba and Greg stood in the check-in line until 1:30. Only two other people were there. Where was the staff?

The plane was supposed to leave in thirty minutes! They located an official who said the plane was delayed until 3:30. Great. But at least there was a plane. We continued to wait, but no one showed up. As the time for the flight came and went, we were told that the plane had decided to continue on to its next destination instead of landing in Lomé.

Jim shook his head. "Yup, that happens. It costs money for them to land, and ten people weren't worth their while. Don't worry, I have a place for you at the guesthouse, and I'll arrange meals. We can try to book a flight out in a couple days."

That night, we had an enjoyable time in comfortable apartments. The next day, Csaba and the kids went to the ocean, and the others headed for the tourist market. I stayed behind for a much-needed rest. This God-arranged delay was a blessing.

On the new departure date, two days later, we went to the airport at 12:30 p.m. for the 2:05 flight. Jim said that the airport opened at 1:00 p.m. . . . *usually*. I asked him what that meant, and he said, "Well, they open when they want to, and no one knows when that will be."

We waited as one o'clock came and went. We started taking bets for a Coke regarding when they would open the doors. Julie said one 1:45, but I, the eternal optimist, guessed 3:00 . . . *after* our plane left, if it came at all. Julie won, and we went inside. This time, we didn't tell Jim to leave. Csaba checked our bags as the rest of us waited by the empty check-in stands.

As the time ticked by, we wondered if this plane, too, was only theoretical. Finally, hours later, we were able to board and were bumped up to first class to compensate for the wait. First class meant we got a slightly larger seat a few rows up and were served a questionable sandwich. The people in coach only got drinks, so we were thrilled.

As we flew, I looked down at the plantations and villages floating beneath us. I loved Africa, my second home.

At some point, it dawned on me that we were following the coast and not heading north toward Mali. Then I realized, with some alarm, that we were flying back to Ivory Coast! They had failed to tell us at the airport about the connecting flight. It was disturbing to be going back to the same place we had had so much trouble escaping from. Csaba tried to reassure me that we would stay on the plane, but that was not to be.

Thoughts of another plane failing to show and having to be evacuated all over again filled my head while we waited inside the Abidjan airport. We could see foreign troops walking around outside with their machine guns. The connecting flight was supposed to take us to Mali in an hour, but would it? As we waited, Csaba called Josias back at the Abidjan administration center, "Surprise! We're back. You might need to pick us up, so we'll keep you posted." Josias was indeed surprised. Csaba told him that we were surprised, too, and asked him to call Robert and tell him where we were.

By now, I was so weak that I had a desperate feeling that I couldn't keep myself in an upright position. I anxiously looked for a place to lie down on the crowded, dirty airport floor, but there was none. I slumped over in my chair and leaned my head against Csaba.

After an hour or so, we did get on another plane. As we flew north at night, we noticed how dark it was below us. Apparently, the rumor that the south had cut power to the north was true.

We arrived in Mali and were again ushered into a long customs line. In front of us was an African man with six wives all dressed in flowing white robes. They looked wealthy. The ladies were quite vocal in expressing their opinions to him often and all at once. I wondered how he managed them all.

Soon we were free to get our baggage and found Robert waiting for us at the other end. We were relieved that our dangerous ordeal was over at last.

Chapter 6

Bamako, Mali

> The great master Gardener, the Father of our Lord Jesus Christ, in a wonderful providence, with His own hand, planted me here, where by His grace, in this part of His vineyard, I grow; and here I will abide till the great Master of the vineyard think fit to transplant me. (Samuel Rutherford)

EVERYONE WELCOMED US WARMLY AT the guesthouse in Bamako, thankful we had made it. As people listened to our news, I was in danger of collapsing with fatigue and had to try hard to hold myself upright. But I was thankful I was in a place where I finally *could* collapse. I was looking forward to resting without having to flee again afterward. Everyone was wonderful to us, and over the next week the missionaries brought us meals and tried to provide us with whatever we lacked. We were grateful to them and to all who helped along the way, and to our great God who is Lord over all.

We were later told by one of the missionaries that when all of us refugees arrived in Mali, we looked completely flattened, both physically and emotionally. They prayed for us during this recovery time, and over the next couple of months the rest of the group slowly got the bloom of life back. I wanted badly to join them, but although I had expectations that I would pull up soon, it would take me six more years to come back from the dead.

My hopes of recovery started to slip away when I fell ill with the seasonal flu. The ground I had gained I lost again, and then some. It was like trying to climb a steep set of stairs out of a deep cavern. If I overdid it or got sick, I slipped back down many steps, and I would have to climb them all over again just to get to the same place. The top was almost out of sight for me. I was determined to get there somehow, one step at a time, but I was starting to realize that this could take a very long time.

When things go better than expected, people say, "God is so very good." When things end up being much harder than we planned, we need to say that God is *still* so very good. He is always good, because He is God. Either He is who He says He is, or He is not. With that knowledge, we can look up daily in faith to see His goodness no matter which way He chooses to write our story. Yes, the evacuation period was hard, but God was using it to prepare us for different types of storms to come.

The kids seemed happy. Even though they grieved the loss of their home in the village, they were adapting well to the new environment, finding new friends and new things to do.

In spite of the gifts from the other missionaries, we still needed clothes, so Csaba went to the open market for used clothing and outfitted us as best he could. Then he bought some cloth which he took to a tailor to make the rest of what we needed.

We were in a furnished apartment and were thankful to have as much as we did. I sorely missed our schoolbooks but was able to use some which had been left behind by other missionaries. I think what we missed most was our personal Bibles, which had been too heavy to bring in our evacuation bags. Months later, some of us got our Bibles back when Alexis arrived from Ivory Coast to work with Csaba. He also brought Noai's art supplies and her violin. God was providing.

Our apartment in Bamako was on the second floor of Wycliffe's administration center and comfortable enough except that the sun baked the walls during the day, causing the temperature inside to rise to 99 degrees Farenheit.

With temperatures soaring to 115 degrees outside, even the tap water was warm.

Many months later, we would move to a house behind the center that we rented from another missionary family on furlough. That house had a swamp cooler we could run as much as we wanted. It also had a beautiful yard enclosed by a wall covered with bougainvillea cascading down in a pink waterfall of blossoms. A vaulted ceiling of fig trees swept the sky above, while below was a swimming pool bordered by tropical plants.

But until we moved to that house, we had to endure the strength-sapping heat in the apartment. We had fans to help, but the one air conditioner was too expensive to run, so it remained largely unused. Instead, we dipped our curtains in water and ran fans on them. It reduced the inside temperature to 94 degrees, which made things tolerable if you didn't move much.

At the end of our first month in Bamako, I was still hoping to recover my strength after that initial bout of flu. Instead, it was like I had an ongoing flu, even though the illness was technically over. The crushing fatigue and weakness confined me to bed most of the time. Normally an active, social person who loves being busy and out and about interacting with people, I hated having to stay down. I could hardly wait to be functioning again, even if it was at a low level. I wanted to get back on my feet to relieve Noai of the cooking because, after all, it was my job. She was cheerful, didn't complain, and her cooking was wonderful. I have often wondered where we would have been in those years without Noai.

As Christmas approached, we were looking forward to seeing Hans again, but it dawned on us that we had no tree, no decorations, and no presents. God provided again, and we were given a fake tree. We made our own Hungarian decorations of two candies wrapped in tinfoil and ruffled paper, tied to each other with long ribbons, and slung over the tree branches. We were able to buy a few other Christmas things as well, and, bless him, Hans brought presents from the States that I had asked him to order.

When Hans arrived, the fun began. The kids made elaborate paper airplanes and flew them off the balcony of the covered roof. They played their instruments on a Saturday morning, waking up our personnel director who lived in the apartment directly below us. They got into a massive rubber-band fight at their friends' house, turning their living room into a war zone. Hans even formed a Coke bottle band by filling the bottles with different levels of water and blowing into them to play "When the Saints Go Marching In."

Sometimes the children joined the Mali missionary Celtic band on the roof of the center. As I watched them play in the cool of the evening, I could see the Niger river in the distance, with the lights of Bamako twinkling softly on the horizon. Occasionally, I could even see a dugout canoe floating by. I enjoyed this typical African scene while listening to Celtic music played by American, Irish, and British missionaries. That was what we liked—culture in any form, and sometimes all mixed together.

After Christmas, Hans returned to the States, and the rest of us settled back into our daily routines. Csaba worked at the office on the Bible translation, the kids did their schoolwork, and Noai cooked in the evenings. Over the next month or so, Csaba took the kids to church on Sundays, but I was still too weak to sit up for that long. I missed going to church. I missed the busyness of daily life as well. I loved being out and about, and after months of being shut in, I felt discouraged. Csaba read up on chronic fatigue and discovered that having a steady routine that didn't vary was important to recovery, which meant we should only add activities back slowly to allow my body time to adjust.

This new trial was tough, but Csaba continued to encourage me in it. "A lot has happened that has been hard, and it is easy to focus on all that's been taken away. So let's thank God right now for what we still have."

I was all in favor of doing this, but after being thankful that we were all *alive*, I struggled to think of much else to thank God for. I had a flu-like feeling that never went away, and I was mostly confined to my bed or the couch. I was grieving the loss of our home in the village, and I missed the lush tropical green of Ivory Coast. It was so very hot in our apartment in the desert country of Mali.

I was not starting well, so Csaba said, "OK, I'll help you. Do you have a bed?"

"Yes" (even though it was a thin, old mattress that I touched bottom with).

"OK, that is a good thing. Let's thank God for that, since many Africans don't have mattresses and have to sleep on mats." That was true, so I thanked God for my bed.

Then he said, "Do you have a pillow?" I acknowledged that as well. "Many Africans don't have that luxury, either, so this is another good thing. Let's thank God for that."

I could see his point. Once I got started, I found that I had *a lot* to be thankful for, like the fact that we had an apartment ready for us when we arrived (albeit a hot one), with the morning sun streaming through the windows and casting pretty light patterns around the room. Outside the window, the sun hit the leaves on the trees, lighting them up in brilliant shades of green that twinkled and danced as the wind blew. I thanked God for this beauty and for the many missionaries at the center who were so accommodating. I was especially thankful for my best friend and husband who took such good care of me. He was an amazing blessing. The children were also wonderful. *Remembering* seemed to be the key to keeping perspective—recounting the many blessings I still enjoyed as well as not forgetting God's goodness, His promises, and His presence. Contentment in any situation is first a *choice*; then it becomes a process as we change our thought patterns to match God's. I had to train myself on this.

Chapter 7

Life in Mali

> I thought it had been an easy thing to be a Christian, and that to seek God had been at the next door, but oh, the windings, the turnings, the ups, and the downs that He hath led me through! And I see yet much way to the ford. (Samuel Rutherford)

WE WOKE TO LOUD SHOUTING AROUND midnight. Alarmed, we looked out the window, which was two stories above the street, and saw mobs of people in the nearby Togolese bar, smashing glass, destroying things, and carrying stolen items away. Looking down, we saw a couch with legs underneath walking by below us.

Frightened, I asked Csaba if they were going to break into the center and whether we should flee to the roof. Csaba wasn't sure what was happening, so he turned on the radio and found it was just anger over a soccer game to qualify for the Africa Cup. Mali had lost to Togo, so the crowds were only targeting the Togolese.

It was still frightening, but at least Jeremiah and Noai slept through the whole thing. Andreas woke up thinking he was back in Abidjan, until we reminded him that we were in Mali, and the crowd was not after us. I felt sorry for the Togolese, knowing what it felt like to be the target of this kind of violence. As the evening progressed, the mob smashed most of the streetlights in our area. The entire situation was unexpected, since normally Mali is such a calm country.

Following that unexpected "storm," actual thunderheads began rolling in with the start of the wet season. We were out on the covered roof one day when a violent tempest whipped in with fury. We always loved watching a good thunderstorm in all its horrible glory, but this one began just after Noai's Malian friend and her mother had decided to pay us a visit. They were escorted to our apartment, and Noai and I went down to serve tea.

As we sat in the living room politely exchanging the news with our guests, we witnessed the rain whipping past the windows at a tremendous rate. We had to talk loudly to be heard over the howling of the storm as the tea heated up. I saw something flash by the window and wondered what it was. It did it again, yet I still had no inkling what it could be. The third time it flashed past, I recognized Jeremiah sliding by on the wet tiles of the veranda. As we drank tea and chatted with our guests, Jeremiah whipped by the window again, but this time there was a second blur close behind, and we chanced to see Noai's Irish friend Stephany following Jeremiah's lead. She stopped long enough to beam us a smile, then disappeared back into the torrent.

We kept talking and drinking, when suddenly the completely-soaked outline of Andreas filled the door. He yelled to Noai to come out and enjoy the storm, unaware that she had visitors. She yelled back over the roar that she couldn't. He didn't hear and repeated, "It's fantastic! Come on out!" When Noai had successfully communicated that she was not available, he disappeared into the rain. Noai's guests left when the storm abated. She finally went outside, but by then had missed it all.

ALEXIS

In January, Alexis came to Bamako to work with Csaba for a month. To get there, he took his first plane trip ever. It was really something, especially when the plane took off and flew directly out over the ocean in the direction of America! To his immense relief, the plane soon banked and headed north to Mali.

It was fun having Alexis in Bamako. He ate with us every day during his stay. He had a little culture shock when he came to dinner one night and found Csaba making pancakes. He asked with hesitation what those things in the frying pan were. Alexis couldn't believe we actually ate those *sponges* for a meal! That night, Csaba had to fix him something else instead.

Alexis saw with some dismay that I was still not doing well. He told Csaba that it had been keenly impressed on his mind how we sacrificed for what we did, and he could see what a heavy toll bringing the gospel to the Bakwé had taken on us. He was amazed that we kept coming back. This had given him a new perspective on the work and a more solid will to continue on.

Together, Csaba and Alexis worked on the translation of the Gospel of John. Csaba was able to concentrate on the work even though I was unwell because Noai ran the kitchen and the boys helped with chores. We appreciated our children's cheerful help very much. Csaba and Alexis worked hard the entire month, and at the end, twelve chapters were ready to be formatted and printed. The first printing of the Bakwé dictionary was also awaiting final corrections. Alexis would come again later to work with Csaba on revising the Gospel of John and addressing the computer problems that kept shutting programs down.

LOSS

One day, Csaba found out that the San-Pédro CMA guesthouse where we had stayed during the uprising had been given to the national church since so many of the CMA missionaries had pulled out due to the war. This news was a blow because that place had been so special to us, a home away from home. It felt like the end of an era. Csaba reminded everyone that God had given us many years in Ivory Coast, and no one could take those memories away. In fact, a lot of memories were already tucked away in my first two books.[1] I reminded everyone that at least we had been able to see the guesthouse again before it closed. We wanted things to stay the way they had been in their glory years, with all the people and places we had known and loved still there. God was closing doors, and as He did, we grieved and said goodbye to each one.

In C.S. Lewis' book *The Last Battle*, Narnia's lights go out one by one as the whole world disintegrates. That's how I found myself feeling about the Ivory Coast. Its lights were going out, and our lives in it were ending before we wanted them to. We weren't ready for that yet. I also wasn't ready for the fact that I now had a body that didn't work.

As I thought about these things, I felt overwhelmed with sadness. I went to the sink and turned on the faucet to let the soothing water run over my hands. As the water flowed, I absentmindedly cupped my hands, filling them up. As the water flowed into and over my hands, I opened them, letting the water spill out before cupping my hands again.

1. *At The Edge of the Village* (Canon Press, 2003) and *From the Village to the Ends of the Earth* (Canon Press, 2020).

I repeated this many times as I dwelt on all the loss we had experienced. Then I wept. So much that had been in our hands had been taken away.

But then I started focusing on the water. When I cupped my hands, the water filled the void right up and seemed to chuckle, gurgle, and laugh in the process, as if nothing could stop its joy. It was such a happy sound; it felt so good and so alive, like the type of life that only the Lord can give.

I did this again and again, until it felt as if God were intruding into my thoughts asking, "What are you doing?"

"Filling my hands with water and letting it go."

"What happens when you let the water go?"

"My hands fill up again."

No matter how often I let the water go, my hands never remained empty because they were being filled by a source that would never stop. Suddenly, I felt God's comfort all around me, His understanding and nearness to His child who was hurting so badly. I knew that even when I saw hands that were empty for the moment, God's love would never stop refilling and overflowing. No matter how much was taken out of my hands, God would always fill them up again.

> But whoever drinks of the water that I shall give him will never thirst. But the water that I shall give him will become in him a fountain of water springing up into everlasting life. (John 4:14)

Chapter 8

Searching for Answers

> If your Lord calls you to suffering, be not dismayed; there shall be a new allowance of the King for you when ye come to it. One of the softest pillows Christ hath is laid under His witnesses' head, though often they must set down their bare feet among thorns. (Samuel Rutherford)

HUNGARY

In February 2005, we received an email from Csaba's parents offering to take the whole family to Hungary for their 50th wedding anniversary in June. We had always wanted to see Hungary as a married couple since Csaba's father came from there, but we had never had the money or the time to do so.

The email included an itinerary for the trip. We saw a picture of the bed and breakfast we'd be staying at, and it looked amazing! Csaba's dad talked about the places we would go, restaurants we would eat at, and pastry shops we'd visit. It was a dream come true, a pleasant reward to look forward to. I began to concentrate on making it through the intervening months to reach the point when we could go to Europe for a break and escape from the heat, the suffering, and the news of war.

After a few more months of my body still not responding to rest, I realized that I could not go. Csaba recognized it, too. I wasn't even strong enough to go see a doctor yet, let alone be wheeled onto an airplane. I needed strength that I didn't have. I went back into the bedroom and told Csaba, "I can't do this. You know I can't do this." Then I broke down and wept.

Csaba wanted to stay behind with me, but I felt strongly that he should go with the kids, since we were not likely to get this chance again. It would be good for them to celebrate with the extended family who would be there, and with Hans who was making the trip from the United States. (Missing the chance to see him was the hardest thing about having to stay behind.) It was also dawning on me that I would not have the strength to go back to Ivory Coast if it were to open up again. This meant that once we returned to the States, we would have to stay there until I got better—if I ever did.

As I wept there in the bedroom, I thought, "Why is it that those who need something the most are often denied it? Why, after all the losses, do I have to stay in bed to reflect on this grief with a mind that can't even think straight, let alone process it all? Why am I always cooped up when I need fresh air, the beauty of nature, something positive to experience, and the fellowship of others? And why is the thing I was looking forward to the most (seeing Hans) to be denied me, especially after such intense trials?"

Csaba held me like he always did and then, with sympathy in his eyes, encouraged me with the kind of comforting words from Scripture that he always spoke at just the right moment. He told me to focus on our full hands of God's faithfulness and love, instead of an empty hand of my momentary dashed desires.

After he left, I opened the Bible at random. My eyes fell on this passage: "But Zion said, 'The Lord has forsaken me, and my Lord has forgotten me.' Can a woman forget her nursing child, and not have compassion on the son of her womb? Surely they may forget, yet I will not forget you. See, I have inscribed you on the palms of My hands; Your walls are continually before Me" (Isa. 49:14–16).

Reading these words, I was filled with a deep thankfulness for the living water that would never stop running in my soul. No matter what desert God put me in, there would always be an internal oasis trickling, bubbling, laughing, and roaring—never stopping. *The Lord had not forgotten me.*

Csaba and the kids had a lovely time in Hungary but missed me, as I did them. When they returned, the kids showed me all the things they had bought. It made me glad that they could experience it all. They learned more about their heritage and even played their instruments in the public square in front of a castle tower they visited. I hoped that one day God would allow me to go, too. But first we needed some answers to the mystery of my chronic fatigue.

THE DOCTOR VISIT

I was finally (barely) strong enough to handle a trip to the doctor's office. After braving the crazy traffic of Bamako, we found the medical building. Inside, fatigue swept over me. We sat down, and I leaned my head against Csaba's shoulder to rest as we waited in the hot and stuffy lobby. After what seemed an interminably long time, we were called in.

The Malian doctor was older and had large, gentle eyes but was every inch a character. He asked me what was wrong, and I told him that I had been unusually tired this past year. He blurted out, "Well that doesn't surprise me. How long have you been in Africa? It is a very harsh life you've lived up till now, and at your age [I was in my 40s] you ain't no spring chicken anymore! Being tired doesn't surprise me a bit. You're just worn out. You've had quite the shock with the evacuation. You might consider changing your work and staying in the States."

After giving us that novel information, he ordered some lab tests, and we left. At the follow-up visit, we again waited in the heat. After an hour, my strength was slipping, and I felt like I needed to be lying down. I found it ironic that the process of seeing a doctor was reserved for those strong enough to do it. When we finally got into the room, the doctor asked us for the test results. We told him that *he* was supposed to have the results. The lab technician had informed us, and the receptionist had assured us, that the doctor would have the results. The doctor quickly called the lab at the medical school and told them that the head doctor was to call him back *en case d'urgence!*—right away! Then he told us to return to the lobby and wait while he saw another patient.

Half an hour later, and me much weaker, we were called back into his office to learn that no results had come yet. The doctor said that from what he could see, there was nothing wrong with me, and if I kept pulling up, I could stay on in Africa for the year. He went on to say that our work was important, but not so important as to be worth jeopardizing my health. I was too young to be feeling so old, and living in Africa really did wear a person down.

As he was saying this, the nurse kept coming into the room to tell him this or that. Getting frustrated at the string of interruptions, the doctor said with some agitation, "How can I talk when I keep getting interrupted!? Ah, these people! I know what I'll do. I'll just *lock* the door so they can't come in." *Click.* "Like that!" With a flick of his wrist, he locked all the nurses and other irritants out and went back to pleasantly chatting with us, his guests. During our conversation, the doorknob behind us continued to rattle—presumably the nurse trying to get back in.

Finally, the lab results arrived. The doctor said in a satisfied manner, "Ah, I knew they would come through. You see, they are my students, and they'll do anything for me."

The results were all negative. The doctor wanted me to do a parasite test to make sure nothing was lurking, but I was adamantly against it because I knew it would entail driving to the far side of the city, waiting to get in at the lab, then driving all the way back through heavy and erratic traffic. I felt so horrible after going anywhere that this option wasn't appealing. But the doctor insisted, and he was not to be denied.

The parasite tests proved negative as well. On paper, I was healthy. This was not necessarily good news, because I really was not well. We just didn't know what was wrong.

Both we and the elders of our sending church realized that I could no longer handle the harsh life of Africa unless God healed me. During a conference call, our church suggested we consider coming home right away because of my health. Csaba explained that we would have to wait until I was strong enough to travel. At the moment, I was too weak to be wheeled onto an airplane, let alone make the whole trip home.

Since the situation in Ivory Coast prevented us from going back there while I recovered enough to travel back to the States, the elders talked about how to run the translation project from afar while we were in Mali, which would mean buying a satellite modem to communicate with the team in the village via email. They also talked about having someone from the church come out to help us set up the modem and troubleshoot the problems.

We were well aware of the precarious state of the translation project, which was facing a myriad of challenges. At the moment, the Bakwé team's time was taken up with their own issues of keeping their families safe, and we didn't know if or when they would have time to resume work. Even if everyone stayed safe, our office and home back in the village could be ransacked and our important equipment taken. We had heard of other projects whose teams had lost years' worth of work in a war. We would just have to trust God to overcome these difficulties each step of the way to bring His Word to the Bakwé.

Chapter 9

Cook Wanted

FRIDAY WAS A MUSLIM HOLIDAY. THE loudspeaker on the mosque droned its chants while we attempted to homeschool, and I was not appreciating the background music. After an hour or two, the droning stopped, and we went up on the covered roof. Below, in every courtyard, people were butchering rams and braising the meat over fires. The smell of roasted ram was all over town, and it made us want some, but we had chicken that day.

Speaking of food, we still needed a cook! I really wanted Noai to have a more manageable load. There is a big difference between the fun of cooking occasionally and the full load of feeding a family under trying conditions. Noai had done admirably. Cooking is a way of bringing a little bit of heaven to our world, a bit of beauty to our everyday lives through taste, and Noai brought that beauty to us. Occasionally, I tried to get in the kitchen and take over, but I was too weak. I felt bad that my trial was affecting others, but I also had to realize that God meant it to be that way. He hadn't given the trial only to me, but to them as well. In giving it to all of us, He meant it for a blessing, not a curse. As Noai rose to the challenge of cooking for the family, God was using her to bless us and was blessing her in the process.

But African cooks were not easy to find. The one Csaba had engaged ended up being almost theoretical. She missed work so much that it was like we had no cook at all. We tried to hire a different cook, and were waiting to hear back. In the meantime, Noai was back at the post, but she didn't seem to mind. Since the situation couldn't be changed, I had the idea of using it to her advantage. Part of Noai's coursework for her senior year of high school had been left behind in Ivory Coast. She needed something to make up the missing work, so I added a course on cookery using *The Joy of Cooking* as our text. Noai read through the book and prepared a recipe from each section. She also made her own cookbook with entries from each category and added ten original recipes. As a final project, she put on a fancy dinner using what she had learned. We benefited greatly from this course of study!

Well, wonders never cease, and we were finally able to get some house help to take on the cooking and cleaning. The blessing of having assistance was not without its interesting moments. For example, one day my floor got mopped with Listerine mouthwash. It was my fault, of course—I had failed to specify what exactly I wanted my floors washed *with*! Another time, I walked into the bathroom and found our worker conscientiously cleaning the toothbrushes with Comet. I really had to think of all the ways I did *not* want things cleaned and let the help know first.

On my birthday, I was told that Noai was in the kitchen cooking me a birthday meal while I lay in bed. At one point, I went out to see how she was doing and saw that it was 99 degrees Farenheit in the kitchen. I couldn't believe it. She was busy in all that heat cooking something to make my day special. That really touched me. I was extremely grateful to God for my daughter.

Another gift was just how funny my kids could be when they interacted with each other. One day, Noai found a daffodil-yellow glue stick (the non-toxic kind). It looked an awful lot like Chapstick. Noai took that glue stick and pretended to use it on her lips. Then she walked over to Andreas, who was concentrating on something else, and handed it to him saying, "Here." Andreas took it and, out of habit, applied it to his lips. Once it dawned on him what had just transpired, he howled and lunged at Noai, who conveniently disappeared around a corner, giggling. A grand chase with much laughter ensued.

Then there was the time Noai was practicing her vibrato exercises on the violin in her bedroom. It sounded an awful lot like a giant mosquito. The continued repetitions began to drive the household crazy. I heard Andreas, who was practicing his uilleann pipes[1] in the other room, shout, "Kill it!" He burst into Noai's room, flipped his chanter up into the *spray* position, and sprayed the Noai "mosquito" with a loud blast of noise. The blast went on for a full minute, as if he was emptying a can of Raid on a giant insect. It worked, because Noai stopped her exercises long enough to ask him what on earth he thought he was doing.

THE ART OF MAKING MALIAN TEA

One afternoon, I went to wade in the courtyard pool at the new house that we were renting behind the apartment buildings, and Noai came out with her little charcoal burner and metal teapot to make Malian tea for me. She lit the coals in the burner and fanned them into life. Once they were ready, she put tea leaves, sugar, and water in the metal teapot and then placed it on the burner. Andreas came and sat next to her with our new parrot on his shoulder. As he watched Noai wait for the water to boil, Andreas had questions. "Noai, why do you do this? It takes you half an hour to make one batch of tea. Why not just heat the water on the stove?"

Noai replied in her patient, older-sister tone, "That's just the way it is done here. There's a finesse, a culture, and a

---

[1]. Irish bagpipes, pronounced *IL-ən*

beauty to it. You're supposed to sit with other people and chat while you make tea in your courtyard. Everyone does it that way."

She took the teapot off the charcoal burner. Holding the pot a foot above the little shot glass, she poured the tea out, trying to hit the small glass below. This process of pouring from a height gives the tea the characteristic frothy texture that the Malian people so dearly love. Again, the commentator spoke up. "Noai, you just poured half the tea on the ground!"

She calmly responded, "No, just one fourth this time. I'm getting better! Do you want to try doing it, Mr. Smarty-Pants?" He didn't.

After repeating this procedure multiple times until the tea was sufficiently foamed, she put it back on the burner to reheat. When it was done, Andreas was offered the first glass of bittersweet, frothy tea. Despite his comments about the production, he liked it. He always did.

AN OUTING TO THE CLIFFS

Csaba decided that he would take off work whenever I felt even the slightest bit up for an outing. A day arrived when I felt a little bit better. Csaba dropped everything, and we headed out.

We wove through traffic like a boat on a conflicting current. Around us flowed a fast-moving stream of cars, trucks, pedestrians, and donkey carts all trying to go somewhere at the same time. This current broke out into rapids as cars and trucks made bold attempts to cross lanes. When the river of vehicles started to pile up behind a donkey cart, everything came to a standstill until the donkey moved, and the mad rush continued downstream once more.

As we reached the edge of the city, the flow of traffic slowed to a gentle current with only one car ahead of the other. We passed shops, stands of fruit, and more donkey carts before turning off the main road and past a few scattered houses at the edge of the wooded savannah. Driving into the countryside, we followed a plantation of old mango trees until the road stopped by a muddy pond at the foot of some cliffs. The children jumped out of the car and dashed up the cliffs with their instruments. Csaba and I sat down under a spreading mango tree by the pond to enjoy the cool of the shade. I lay down on the rock and rested my head in Csaba's lap. It felt so good to be out of the bustle of the city and in the peace and beauty of this arid, rocky place. In the sky, an eagle soared above the cliffs, and I followed his flight with my binoculars.

Two Fulani herdsmen wandered by to let their cows drink from the pond. When they finished, they passed through the scattered shrubbery and out of sight. All we needed was someone playing the cora[2] to add to this African pastoral scene. Instead, I heard Celtic music wafting from

---

2. A traditional Malian stringed instrument

above. I looked up and saw Noai and Andreas silhouetted against the sky, sitting on the edge of the cliff and playing their whistles while Jeremiah stood beside them.

After a while, the kids came down, and we walked back to the car. On the way, I spied a beautiful bloom that had sprung up out of the barren ground. It was only a flower with nothing else, not even leaves. I wondered how something so delicate and beautiful could thrive in such rocky ground. It reminded me of how a Christian can blossom in the harshest conditions, since God's indwelling presence is their source of life. I thought to myself, "I want to be like that flower."

Chapter 10

The Bakwé Team

IN SEPTEMBER 2005, THE BAKWÉ TRANSlation team came up to Mali to help Csaba check the Gospel of John with our translation consultant, Renée Vick, an American missionary working with Wycliffe. Bart, a volunteer from our village, came as a back translator, someone who orally translates the Bakwé translation back into French so the consultant can ask questions. This role was new to Bart. He wanted to go beyond the questions at hand and had to be reminded that Renée was not testing his Scripture knowledge but only that the text was translated correctly. The checking went well, and they finished the Gospel of John in two weeks. The team spent the remainder of the time making corrections and preparing the epistles of 1, 2, and 3 John for checking. After that, they hoped to finish James and start on Galatians.

That night, I served hamburgers, which Alexis loved but evidently Bart did not. The next night, we decided to provide something Ivorian instead. Greasy rice (an African version of paella) fit the bill. But our cook chose to embellish the greasy rice with things Malian. From the living room, I smelled an awful stench. I went to the kitchen to find out what had died. Not discovering any deceased creatures in there, I asked our cook what was that *awful* smell? He said it was probably the fish that he had added to flavor the sauce. I asked if the fish was rotten, and he replied that, why yes, as a matter of fact it was. The Malians have a special dish that includes fermented fish, a flavor they love. Missionaries had warned us about this dish, and I had hoped never to experience it.

I asked our cook if he could please take the fish bits out of the simmering sauce. He looked a bit hurt and told me they added to the flavor. I told him that, really, I was not crazy about this fish in the sauce. He scooped the pieces out, but the odor remained.

As we were eating, I poked at something unidentifiable in the rice. I went to the kitchen to ask the cook what it was. "Snails." I thanked him for that bit of info and left. The rest of the meal was pretty good. Csaba reminded me that it would take our cook a while to figure out what we did and did not like, and we needed to have patience with each other in the meantime.

We had other cultural differences with the household help as well, including what constituted beauty. Noai likes dried flower arrangements, and she had preserved some flowers by hanging them upside down to dry. When they were dry, she put them in a vase. Seeing the dead flowers, our Malian cook dutifully threw them out. When Noai found the vase empty, she ran to the garbage to rescue her dried flowers and put them back in the vase. Our conscientious worker saw that the dead flowers had mysteriously reappeared and threw them out again.

When Noai saw that they had disappeared a second time, she retrieved them again and put them back in the vase. I don't know how long this would have gone on, but the third time Noai saw the empty vase, she ran out to the yard, only to find that her dried flower arrangement had gone to the dump with the 9:00 a.m. donkey express.

I explained to our Malian cook that in America, when we are done with fresh flowers, we sometimes turn them upside down, let them dry, and put them back in the vase as a decoration. He looked at me in astonishment. I explained to him that in America we think dead flowers are pretty. He shook his head incredulously but assured me that should he find dead flowers in a vase again, he would let them be.

CHRISTMAS 2005

Hans and his friend Benjamin came out to Mali for Christmas. Benjamin was from our home church in Idaho and brilliant with the computer, so he volunteered to help Csaba during his time with us. Csaba was glad for his assistance converting the fonts in our old files into the latest font standard. Many of the files were publications that would need to be reprinted in the future. Rather than converting the fonts one file at a time, Benjamin was able to run the conversion on batches of files, making the process go much faster.

When Benjamin wasn't working with Csaba, the kids had fun playing music together. Hans had been the drummer and Benjamin the guitarist for Dol Baran, their old Celtic band back in Idaho. Andreas and Noai were thrilled to play with them again on their whistles but were not used to their fast pace. I chanced to see them playing together one day. Benjamin was strumming wildly on his guitar with the whistles trailing frantically behind, when he stopped abruptly, looked up at the others, and said, "I won."

I have always appreciated the music in our house and just love it when the kids play together. The evacuation from Ivory Coast had been much easier to bear because their music accompanied us everywhere we went. As Noai wrote in an essay for her classwork,

> To drain the world of music would be like draining its very blood . . . Go for a walk and you will

be struck with how much music runs in the veins of our world. Everything is flowing in music. The birds sing...to the Lord. The trees dance to a song only they can hear—the wind. A brook babbles happily on its way through a green mossy wood plucking on its clear, watery harp. The very growth of plants shows their Creator's song working in them. *Creation is packed full of music.* Each thread of life has its own song which, when woven into the great tapestry of creation, comes together to make one harmonious symphony. Music is the mark of God's character and craftsmanship in this world, and we, being part of this creation, should be in harmony with it.

After a wonderful stay with us, Benjamin and Hans returned to the States.

IVORY COAST WOES

In January 2006, Ivory Coast was in a state of upheaval again. It seemed like the president was backing out of the peace process entirely. If he did, a return to open war would be the only way to resolve the situation. We felt a fresh wave of grief at this news, which also dashed our hopes of returning to our Ivorian home. We grieved for what was happening to the country, especially all the needless death. We grieved for the suffering the Ivorian people were enduring. And yes, we grieved for the separation from our old home in the village. On top of that was the pressure of an unfinished translation project. We were painfully aware that we still had a job to do, and it wasn't done yet.

The situation weighed heavily on our minds. Could we ever go back? Why did our world keep blowing apart? During the time I was thinking about this, Hans wrote me his thoughts after reading C.S. Lewis' book *Surprised by Joy*. Hans recalled a time when he was young and had been enjoying a good rainstorm in our yard. I had come out and placed a dead chick on a piece of pavement for him to bury. He wrote, "Our baby chicks often die, but seeing the dead, wet chick on the pavement and the pouring rain beating on my umbrella just filled me with a wave of sorrow and that longing for eternity all at once; of death, sorrow, and risen gladness. It's times like these, and in nature beholding some splendor, that sometimes glory, sweetness, and sorrow will meet, and a window will be opened in the heart for a brief moment, with a longing for heaven."

This was such a comfort to me. What was a little suffering in the light of eternity?

Chapter 11
The Final Months

> I know we may say that Christ is kindest in His love when we are at our weakest; and that if Christ had not been to the fore, in our sad days, the waters had gone over our soul. (Samuel Rutherford)

GOING BACK TO THE VILLAGE
In March 2006, Ivory Coast had settled down enough to allow for a quick visit, and Csaba went back for the first time since our evacuation in the fall of 2004. On this trip, the plan was for the team to continue to work on the translation, fix computer issues, and install new software. Csaba would also help the team set up a satellite modem so he could email them more easily when we went back to the States.

Alexis met him in Abidjan, and the two drove out to the village. When they entered it, people called out a hello to Csaba in excited voices. "Saro, ayoo!" (Saro is Csaba's Bakwé name.) Csaba greeted them in return as he drove by. He planned to wait until morning before going to each courtyard to officially greet the people according to custom. But, breaking with custom, the entire village came to him, streaming from all corners to our front yard, singing as they went. Drove after drove of people flocked in with drums and rattles thundering in the background. They had all come to welcome Csaba back after such a long absence. He was overwhelmed at the outpouring of love; he had never seen anything like that before.

Csaba wanted us to experience their welcome, so he called me on his cellphone and let us listen. Hearing the joyful noise, I could just imagine seeing all those familiar faces, sounds, and sites and experiencing the feelings of coming home again with Csaba. It touched our hearts to hear it. When I hung up the phone, I cried because I knew I would not be going back anytime soon, if at all.

When the singing and dancing stopped, it was time to give the news. The people told Csaba how concerned they had been about us when we had to flee. Then they asked where I was. Csaba told them that my health had not been good since we evacuated, and that I had been too weak to come with him. They sympathized with many Bakwé utterances of condolence. They asked how the kids were, and then Csaba asked them for the news of the village. They recounted the suffering they had gone through and the deaths they'd had. They showed him the hole where a bullet had entered the bricks of the Translation and Literacy building during the unrest. Csaba noticed that the village children kept looking for our children to come out of the house and play. He had to keep telling them that our children would not be coming this time.

After the crowd left, Csaba went inside with some of his Bakwé colleagues. Two separate meals of rice and sauce were brought to him. He had a good time of fellowship with his colleagues over dinner. Firmain, a member of the translation team and the pastor of the Bakwé church in our village, told Csaba that the church was thriving. Between thirty and forty kids were coming to Sunday school each week, and many new adults had started attending the service. Even Poto Mathieas' family was coming. He had been the biggest fetisher[1] of the village and the church's main opposition. But before he died a couple years earlier, he had encouraged his family to go to church.[2] Firmain also told Csaba that the

---

1. A fetisher is someone who is involved in sorcery and is believed to have special powers to work charms.
2. After his wife and children became Christians, he saw the change in their lives. When he was dying, he wondered what would happen to them because his fetishes wouldn't be able to protect them anymore after he was dead. But he knew that God must be stronger than all fetishes, so when Sunday came, he encouraged them to go to church. Firmain was visiting him before he died and talked about God. It is possible that he converted on his deathbed.

church had been praying for me every week and would pray even harder, with fasting, asking God for healing.

Later that evening, although he was tired, Csaba went through the house and packed up as many of the books and children's things he could get into the trunks he had brought with him. He knew he had to work at night to get this done, as each day would be filled up with visitors.

The next day very early, according to custom, he went around the whole village to give his greetings. At each house, everyone expressed concern that I was still in Mali and not in the village where I could finally rest and get better. They wanted us to return. Csaba replied that we, too, wished we could come back to the village, but that I needed to go back to my own country to recover. They agreed that I needed to go back to where my mom could cook for me. Annique[3], Alexis' sister, said, "You tell her not to give up. Tell her not to get discouraged. God knows what he is doing." She gave Csaba a bright Ivorian cloth to deliver to me, with these words written on it: *All that God does is good.*

LEAVING AFRICA

In May 2006, I finally had enough strength to make the return trip to the United States if I used a wheelchair, so we started to make plans. Our pastor's wife emailed us to

3. Pronounced *Ah-NEEK*.

say that the church wanted to get our house ready by doing a makeover. She had a budget to work with and asked what type of furniture I wanted since they would be able to buy some new things. I was astounded. As missionaries, we hadn't bought new furniture ever, except at the roadside place in Africa. She showed me an online site, and I was drawn to a style that was very African. She took it from there. I was very thankful for these glad tidings, but at the same time I found myself unable to look forward to the makeover. I thought it would just be another good thing hoped for but taken away at the last minute. After so many dashed expectations, I had quit looking forward to anything. Somehow it seemed easier that way.

As we prepared to leave, Noai was feeling the goodbyes keenly. Africa was her home, and she was saying farewell to it yet again, possibly for the final time, and was dreading it. She wrote in an email to a friend, "There is such a wonderful community here. We are like one big family and can pop over to each other's houses with our teacups in hand. I have my place here. At school, I am a teacher to the little kids, while to the other kids I am their friend and older sister. To the mothers here, I am like one of their daughters. It is wonderful."

The community in Mali had been wonderful, but I was eager to get back to our family and friends in Idaho and to a life with a bit of constancy in it. Chronic, low-level grief had become part of our constantly shifting world. As we said our goodbyes in Mali to another round of people we had come to love but might not see again, I wasn't sure how much more change coupled with grief I could take.

Our truck drove out of the courtyard and down the road, and the old familiar buildings slipped away for the final time into the shadows of the night. As we rounded the corner and the buildings were no more, Noai broke down and cried. I knew it was good for her to cry, and later I would grieve the loss of our African home, too. But sorrow took energy, so for now I shoved that grief back and concentrated on making it to the States.

At the airport, everything was a blur. All that I knew was that I was being wheeled down one aisle and over to another. The sights and sounds of the busy airport drove my energy dangerously low. I tried to rest my mind by zoning out and looking down. I needed to lie down—badly. At one point, the porter wheeled me onto an elevator that Csaba could not enter. I felt panicky being so helpless and separated from him and not knowing where I was going, but thankfully Csaba was there on the other end.

I was wheeled to the base of the airplane. I honestly don't know how I climbed those stairs to get onto the plane, but somehow I did. Once I was seated, exhaustion swept over me in waves, making me feel sick, but at least the plane was a quieter environment, and I was able to doze off. At the Paris airport, where we stopped for the night, another wheelchair arrived. I slumped into it, hardly aware of what was happening around me. At the hotel, I crashed into bed and slept, but not deeply. While I was sleeping, the family went off on the metro to see the city of Paris.

The next day, the flight was long, and it, too, was a blur. When we landed in Chicago, where we were to stay at my parents' place for a bit, another wheelchair was waiting. We went through customs and out the other end, where my parents were waiting for us. They hugged the rest of the family, then came to me. I was slumped in my wheelchair, an emotionless blob, too tired to interact. I was only able to glance up and give them a quick nod. My mom greeted me then fell silent. I felt her eyes examining the crumpled heap that had once been her dynamic daughter, and I could feel her dismay. But I said nothing. I just needed to crash somewhere, and soon. When we got to my parent's house, I went to bed, thankful I had made it. Now I could start to recoup for the final leg of the trip home. It would be a month before I was strong enough to travel again.

My family went on ahead to Idaho to get our house ready. With help from church friends, the walls were painted, the yard put back in order, the house cleaned, the kitchen unpacked, and the sagging carport propped up. As a nice touch, one of the deacons put an overhang on the back door that fit the look of the house perfectly. Nancy, our pastor's wife, arranged her end of the special welcome package by bringing in the new furniture.

FLYING TO IDAHO

After a month, I was strong enough to attempt the trip from Chicago to Idaho, but the journey was problematic because I would have to do it by myself. God would have to help me with His strength, because I certainly did not have enough of my own. We assumed the airlines would provide a wheelchair and assistance for me, which they did, but I hadn't banked on one problem: I was only in my forties and did not look ill.

At the airport, I said goodbye to my parents, thanked them, and was wheeled away. When we arrived at my gate, I was told to get out of the wheelchair. I looked at the porter in dismay. "Can't you wheel me onto the plane? I'm not strong enough to walk hardly at all." He said they didn't do that. I asked him how I was supposed to get on the plane. He said that I'd just have to walk (on my own two legs, like everyone else). Then he turned and left. Not sure what to do, I prayed to God in desperation and turned the problem over to Him. I didn't know how He would solve it, but I knew that He likes to be asked. "Therefore humble yourselves under the mighty hand of God, that He may exalt you in due time, casting all your care upon Him, for He cares for you" (1 Pet. 5:6–7).

I couldn't stand for long without collapsing, but I thought that if I waited to be the last person in line, I could walk straight onto the plane without having to stop and wait. When I tried this, I found to my dismay that the line had stopped midway down the gangplank. I didn't know what to do, so I sat down on the floor of the walkway, leaning my back against the wall, until the line went around the bend. I got up and regained the line, then sat down again, resuming my position against the wall. Sitting and walking, I was able to make it all the way to the door of the plane, where a new problem arose. People were blocking the aisles by stopping to put their luggage in the overhead bins, which meant I had to stand again.

In desperation, I looked around for a place to sit, but there was none, unless I was going to sit on someone's armrest. I stood there in the aisle, sweating it out as the line of people inched forward. As I waited, I stared at the ground, wondering if I shouldn't just sit down in the aisle. Finally, after everyone had their carry-ons stowed, I reached my seat and collapsed with my carry-on still in the aisle.

I stared in dismay at the overhead compartment. There was no possible way I could lift the weight of my suitcase up there with my depleted reserves of strength. The stewardess came by and told me to put my luggage up in the overhead bin right away. I told her I couldn't and asked if she could help me. She said she was not allowed to help and that I needed to do it myself. I told her that I was ill and couldn't get my bag up there. She said she couldn't do it, and would I please get on with it because the plane needed to leave. We were at an impasse since I was unable to do what she asked, so I just sat there.

The stewardess told me again to move my bag out of the aisle or the plane wouldn't leave, and I told her again that I couldn't do it (no matter what the plane did). When the stewardess realized I was in earnest, she said, "Well, maybe someone else can do it for you." Up to that point, everyone sitting near me had been quiet. When it looked like the flight would be delayed due to my bag, some kind gentleman got up and solved the problem by shoving the offending object into the bin with very little effort. I thanked him, then sank back against my seat, relieved. I had lost a lot of energy in that battle with the stewardess, and I still had four hours of flight to go. I gave it to the Lord, then mentally zoned out, not wanting to waste any more energy on future problems than I already had.

In Spokane, a wheelchair was brought to the entrance of the plane, and I was wheeled out to where Csaba was waiting. I don't know when I had been so glad to see him. I could rest now, knowing he would take care of me. I don't remember much after that, except that I couldn't sit up in the car for the ninety-minute drive home, so I lay down across the back seat.

Once home, I entered the house and looked around in amazement. There was a China hutch for dishes and a new kitchen table to replace our old rickety one. There was a new couch and chair in the living room, and a porch table out back. Later, there would be a new bed (the first in our lives) with a nightstand and dresser. The good people of our church had given us this incredible blessing from God, and I couldn't believe it was happening to me! I felt as if God was saying to this pessimist that *if He wanted to bless me, He would do so in His way, and on His time, and my gloomy pessimism was not going to stop the process.*

Chapter 12

Moscow, Idaho

> For I was hungry and you gave Me food; I was thirsty and you gave Me drink; I was a stranger and you took Me in; I was naked and you clothed Me; I was sick and you visited Me; I was in prison and you came to Me.... Assuredly, I say to you, inasmuch as you did it to one of the least of these My brethren, you did it to Me. (Matt. 25:35, 40)

MEREDITH

It was good to be home. I needed to recover from the trip, so I had contact with only a few people at first. I longed to see everyone, but I knew I should wait until I could receive them with something other than a deadpan expression and then telling them they had to leave after ten minutes, which was about my limit. I had already seen Nancy, who had been waiting at the house to welcome me back. I had corresponded with her throughout our time in Africa, and it was good to see her again in person. I also saw Meredith Wilson, my close friend of many years. Meredith knew my situation and offered to help in any way she could.

Being with someone so familiar who knew both me and my condition was a wonderful gift from God. I didn't have to carry on a conversation for the sake of propriety or feel as if I had to explain why I wasn't responding normally. I could just relax while Meredith took over the kitchen, which she did very well. She washed the dishes without my asking and made us tea when I couldn't. She simply understood and got to work. When I became too tired to interact, she would show herself out the door. She was the perfect helper and companion for my current condition.

Meredith is one of those people who never seems to grow old. She zings around the room faster than you can keep track of her. She is always serving, bustling, laughing, and giving—bringing the world to life around her. A seemingly inexhaustible supply of cheerfulness pervades her entire being. Being around her did me much good, as I was greatly flagging in this area. Instead of cheerfulness, I had begun to live in a constant fog of gloom. Meredith's supply of energy and joy made up for my lack, like a prop plane helping to pull a glider off the ground. One of the highlights of my day was picking up the phone and hearing her booming, "Heeeyyyy!" on the other end. How good God was to provide someone like this to minister to me in my isolation! In the years that followed, there were a handful of others who came off and on to visit and help, each one refreshing my soul like cups of cold water in the summer heat.

Meredith checked in every day by phone and visited every other day or so. I thought it was too much for her. She didn't think so. I said I wasn't fun to be around since I could hardly interact. She said I was. I said I wasn't. She said I was, too. We liked to argue! I could not offer her anything in return for her sacrifice or even provide her with interesting conversation since I was often too weak to talk. Her giving was unconditional and from the heart. She was a godsend to help me endure a very difficult season. In the initial years after our return to Idaho, she did more than I can recount or remember, but God knows and will reward her. I was just left with a debt of gratitude.

When I felt up to seeing other people, Meredith gave the word, and it was done slowly. Since my energy could drop unexpectedly, it was hard to schedule a visit in advance. If people came, and I felt myself slipping, I needed to leave the room to lie down in a quiet place, or I could dip dangerously low. I was concerned that visitors wouldn't understand this. After all, *I* didn't even understand it.

Our church, giving as always, provided meals for the family for our first two weeks back. They planned to provide them indefinitely until I got better, but when we realized that I wasn't getting better, Csaba and I knew we needed to figure out how to survive long-term on our own.

WHAT TAKES ENERGY

If you are given only a cup of gas in your gas tank for the whole day, you learn how to dole it out carefully. It is amazing what takes energy. For example, I learned

- It takes more energy to laugh than to cry.
- It takes more energy to sit up than to recline.
- It takes more energy to stand still than to walk.
- It takes more energy to listen to fast music than to slow.

I was surprised by some of the things that took energy: bright or fast-changing lights, facial expression, focusing, processing, concentrating, and making decisions. Groups of people were problematic. Every person added to a group took an additional amount of energy to process, since my ability to sort things out was diminished. A crowded room had a catastrophic effect, short-fusing my brain and plunging me down into exhaustion.

After settling into my new normal, the inevitable day came when my children had to go back to school and

Csaba back to work. Jeremiah and Andreas went to Logos School, Jeremiah in seventh grade and Andreas in ninth. Noai was a freshman at New Saint Andrews College. She loved her classes and was slowly getting used to the culture of America, although she didn't catch on all at once. This became apparent one day when she was sitting in rhetoric class listening to her classmates give speeches. Her feet ached from being confined in shoes, which she wasn't used to wearing, so she slipped them off. She forgot all about it until her professor called her up to give her speech.

When she finished, the professor asked if she had forgotten something. She looked at him in all earnestness and said that no, she didn't think she had. She had given her whole speech.

"What about your shoes?"

She looked down at her bare toes and sheepishly said, "Oops."

Csaba had a space in the building where our church's offices were located. He enjoyed the atmosphere and the people who worked at the heart of the ministry of the congregation. The offices were situated in a semi-circle around a main lobby, which was Chris LaMoreaux's domain. Chris is the church secretary and the most *in the know* person around. She is always aware of what is going on and able to direct you to the right place—the air traffic controller for the church. All flights pass through her. She handles the scheduling so there are no collisions. She is a wealth of information. If you want to know who is getting married or who just gave birth, you ask Chris.

Csaba's office was tucked back around a corner from the lobby and had a large picture window that overlooked the roof of the Chinese restaurant below. He had a folding table for a desk, two computer monitors, multiple Greek texts, Bibles of various translations, and numerous other things a translator needs. The office was lined with bookshelves filled with books and a few African carvings, and a poster board covered with photos from Africa hung on the wall.

Working remotely was not easy. If the internet was running in the village, Csaba would Skype with his team in the mornings (which was their afternoon), and they worked on the translation together. There were frequent interruptions for the team on the other end (family needs, village matters, etc.), but they were able to keep making progress.

Chapter 13

Who Am I?

> Deep in unfathomable mines
> Of never-failing skill,
> He treasures up His bright designs
> And works His sovereign will. (Cowper)

I, IN THE MEANTIME, WAS STILL PRETty much stuck in the prone position. I lay on the couch or my bed most of the day with no relief from the horrible feeling in my body, weighed down by what seemed like a never-ending flu. If this was how my life was going to be from now on, I wanted to live it the best I could. High on my priority list was being *useful* again. I decided to give cooking a try, but after being out of the kitchen for so long, I had almost forgotten how to do it.

My first attempt was pathetic. It was spaghetti with ground beef and a jar of sauce, but it still took hours to accomplish in my state. I pulled up a stool to the stove and sat down. I needed a large spoon, so I reached over to the drawer to get it, but it was missing. I got off my stool and slowly walked across the kitchen to look in another drawer, but didn't find it there, either, so I went back to my stool to rest and ponder my dilemma. After thinking a bit, I shuffled over to the dishwasher and found it! Then I went to the freezer to get some meat to fry. I had trouble finding it. By the time it was found, I was exhausted again, so I went back to my stool and sat down to regain a bit of strength.

Once my energy had risen, I got a frying pan out and then sat down again to recuperate. But then I realized that the meat needed thawing. So I went to get a bowl for the microwave but couldn't find the right one at first and had to look around until I found it. I put the meat in the microwave and sat down, resting my head in my hands while the meat defrosted.

Next, I needed a knife to chop the onion. By this point, I was thinking it would be so nice to have things just fly into my hands by telepathy, but that not being the case, I got a knife, then sat down and rested my head in my hands again. Every time I moved, I felt like I was carrying an invisible five-hundred-pound backpack around the kitchen with me. I fried the meat while slumped over on my stool, barely able to keep myself upright. I needed a jar to pour off the oil from the meat but kept sitting there looking wearily in the direction where the jars were kept, willing them to come on their own. Since they didn't, I went and got one then sat down as I spooned the grease into it. I was so spent by then that I put my spoon down, too tired to think of what to do next. For a long time, I sat there in front of the stove, doing nothing. Finally, I slowly got up and went to lie down on the couch.

The rest of the meal waited until Csaba came home. He greeted me cheerfully, as always, then set to finish the cooking without comment. I was so grateful. Noai continued to help, too, when she could. I was never made to feel guilty for what I couldn't do and was accepted the way I was. But I was having a hard time accepting it myself. How long was this going to last?

As the months passed with no improvement in my situation, a string of questions began to follow me around. Who am I in the grander scheme of things if what I do is taken away from me? Who am I when I seem to have no real purpose or place anymore? What am I when I can't serve others, but others must serve me?

Who am I when I am so weak that my personality is lost in slumber, and I can't provide worthwhile conversation or even show facial expression, let alone speak up to be heard in a group?

Who am I when I sit hunched in a chair off to the side in a room full of people, almost invisible?

What does it mean for my sense of belonging when conversations and smiles fly around in the air above me but don't trickle down below to make me know that I am still valued and worthy of attention? Am I only something pitiful and broken, to be talked to as a duty and not a delight?

Am I losing my sense of *self*? Who am I really?

But, then again, was I asking the right questions?

There was only one question that needed to be asked. All the others hinged on it. *What did God think of me?* The answer was profoundly simple. I was a child of God, an heir of the King. I was His—wanted, loved, and accepted. At the very core of my being and identity, I was His. When that question was answered, *nothing* else really mattered. I believe God wanted me to go through this hard period so that He could show me the power of knowing who I really was in Him when all else seemed to be shaken. "And he who loves Me will be loved by My Father, and I will love him and manifest Myself to him" (John 14:21).

Now that I was in the States, we were hoping for some real answers from the doctors. We went to our general doctor, Dr. Grauke, a fellow member of our church. He ran new tests. After reviewing the data and lab results, he shook his head. Nothing stood out. Then he made a suggestion. "This is a long shot since you don't fit the profile, but you could look into sleep apnea."

We asked what that was. He said it was when you periodically stop breathing during sleep. This deprives your brain and organs of oxygen and can really wreak havoc with your body. We asked him how much the tests would cost. He replied that we would have to get a sleep study at the hospital, and it was pricy. That settled it for us. We didn't have much money to spare and didn't want to spend it on a long shot. Going to the hospital would also wear me out, so we decided to pass.

Chapter 14

Attempting Church

> Ye fearful saints, fresh courage take;
> The clouds ye so much dread
> Are big with mercy and shall break
> In blessings on your head. (Cowper)

I STAYED MOSTLY AT HOME FOR OUR first month in Moscow so I could rest. But I missed going to church. I was very hungry for it. The first Sunday we felt I was up for it, we went. Since we didn't know how long I would last, we left for church late, to reserve as much energy as possible for the service. When we got there, I made a beeline for a seat. Since it was my first Sunday back, people came to where I was sitting to welcome me. Smiling faces with warm greetings touched my heart. The sense of belonging filled me with the thankfulness that this was my church and these were my people. They told me how they had been praying for me, which really encouraged me.

The service started, but I had a sneaking suspicion that I would not last long. All the excitement of the greetings and the sights and sounds of a gymnasium full of people brought on that familiar feeling of slipping down, down into a scary abyss. Soon I realized that I had to get out now if I was to even walk out at all. I nodded to Csaba, and he helped me out on his arm. It had been only eight minutes since the service started. As we left, I felt depressed. I was leaving a grand party before it even properly began. Outside in the still air, everything seemed so silent. And I was going back home to complete silence and isolation.

The Sundays that followed were similar. Each week when my energy gave way, we left through the side door. But at least I was still a part of the congregation, even though I came too late and left too early for much interaction with others. Week after week of attempting to stay just a *little* longer proved fruitless, and I noticed a change in myself that I didn't like. When Csaba led me out into the silent air, I would break down crying. I didn't want to leave, but I didn't know what to do about it. I was way too weak to make it through even to the beginning of the sermon, let alone the whole service and the fellowship time afterwards, but it was becoming too disheartening for me to be led away from it.

I felt like a backpacker who has just finished a long and arduous journey in the mountains in winter and is very weary. This backpacker has experienced much hardship and is looking forward to getting home. As he trudges up the last hill, he sees lights in the castle above and hears the music and laughter of a party going on.

He enters the door and sees a roaring fire on the hearth. The banquet room is brightly decorated with beautiful artwork adorning the walls. People greet him warmly as he passes them. In the center of the room is a table laden with delicacies, and he is so very, very hungry.

Happy people with plates full of food smile as he makes his way to the banquet table. Famished, he reaches out his hand for some food, when suddenly a Presence takes his arm and leads him back out of the room, away from the lights, the table, the food, the people, and the roaring fire. He finds himself back outside in the night, the cold, the silence. Down the steps he goes, over the lawn, and into a small cottage tucked away in the shadows.

The door shuts, and he is alone in a bare, dimly lit room. He walks to the window and looks up at the castle on the hill, with its brightly lit windows and silhouettes of happy people milling about inside. He sighs. There is a banquet up there alright, but it is out of his reach.

Is it possible to starve at a banquet? Yes, if you can't get to the table.

Csaba saw the cloud hanging over me and felt something needed to be done. Since I couldn't be in a sitting position for long, he tried to find a way for me to lie down at church. First, I tried the nursing mom's room that had the sermon piped in. I entered the room, greeted the young moms, then lay down on the floor. That was a bit weird, so I explained my situation, and they nodded. As I tried to listen to the sermon, the conversation amongst the moms drowned it out. Each mom that came in and saw me lying on the tile floor had to be told that I was not having a heart attack. Sometimes you have to take dire measures to go to church, but this one obviously wasn't going to work.

Yet something had to be done, since this was my life now. Csaba brought it up to the elders, and they suggested that I bring a mat and lie down backstage. Our church met in a gymnasium with a stage at one end. The podium was put at the front of the stage, and behind the podium was a thick curtain that concealed the backstage area. This seemed like a great idea, since I could access the curtained area through an offstage entrance. I wouldn't have to leave church and could still get the rest I needed; back in the darkness of the stage I could lie down, resting both body and mind. This would allow me to make it through the service and come out for the Lord's supper before Csaba whisked me off home.

Even though I wasn't sitting with the congregation, now I was *there* at church! Every Sunday for more than a year, I stole up the back steps and onto the darkened stage to lie down on my mat when I could sit up no more. From there, on the other side of the thick curtain, I could hear our pastor preaching.

One week, when I went back to my mat in the darkness, I found a chocolate with a note of encouragement. It was from one of the elders' wives. She had brought a little delight and cheer to me that Sunday!

Each week, from the shadows behind the thick curtain, I listened to our pastor's powerful sermons. They were words of comfort and hope to me, filled with the grace and love of Jesus Christ. They lifted me up to God's presence and gave me the courage to face the week ahead. They let me know that He was still there, and all would come right in the end.

One meditation before the Lord's Supper particularly touched my soul with the promise that God did indeed intend good for me through all of this.

> I have preached often that God provides for his people. "Open your mouth," God says through the Psalmist, "and I will fill it." As parents and grandparents, it delights us when a child in a highchair sees the spoon and dutifully opens his mouth. God delights to feed us. He delights to provide for us. He is the one who sets abundance around us on every

hand, and we are the ones who struggle far too much as we try to understand how intent he is in giving to us, and how doubly intent he is on teaching us how to receive what he gives in all gratitude.

Unbelief in the Scriptures revolves around the strange inability we have to believe that God is going to be good to us, provide for us, and give to us what he promised to give. Even when God calls us to give something up for His sake, it is always because He intends to give us something far more valuable in its place.

And whenever He makes you let go of what you have in your fist, it is because you have nothing but pebbles from the gravel in your driveway. He intends to replace them all with diamonds.

So come, and welcome to Jesus Christ.[1]

I have always liked that word *welcome*. It means you belong; it means you are wanted and loved by Jesus Christ. And since you belong to Him, you also belong to the body of believers. You have a family.

---

[1]. Douglas Wilson, *So Come and Welcome to Jesus Christ* (Moscow, ID: Canon Press, 2007), July 7 entry.

Chapter 15

Trip to Ivory Coast

IN 2007, CSABA WENT BACK TO IVORY Coast for a month, taking with him Kjell[1] Christophersen, a friend and member of our church. Kjell was going to share his economic expertise and life experience (he had lived and worked in Africa for a number of years) by running a small business seminar and setting up a seed fund for loans to help the Bakwé start their own cottage businesses.

Csaba was happy to have a companion and was eager to show Kjell our work. As they drove into the village, the kids surrounded the truck in happy droves. Men and women came running from all corners with shouts of joy. They

---

1. Pronounced *Shell*. You can read more about his adventures in *Memoirs of a Traveling Economist* (Moscow, ID: Canon Press, 2020).

congregated around the stalled truck, hands thrust into the windows to welcome Csaba back and greet Kjell. Then the two continued down the dirt road followed by a crowd of Bakwé kids running behind. At the edge of the village, the truck turned into our yard and went around back, where our workers met them with excited greetings. They grabbed Kjell's and Csaba's bags, and everyone went into the kitchen to get water and exchange news.

The next day, people came in streams to visit. As usual, Csaba was asked where the rest of us were, and he explained that we couldn't come back due to my health. Pastors from town came to greet Csaba and said they were praying for my recovery so that we could all come back home.

When I told Noai about the welcome, she said wistfully, "They still want us. We belong there. We need to get back!"

I reminded her, "We don't belong there right now, because God has placed us here."

Csaba wrote that the house and yard had been well taken care of by Bibionay, our caretaker, and Janvier, our former cook, had made a special effort to come back from his cocoa farm to cook for them. Csaba reported that the teak forest I had planted in 2001 had really grown and was starting to fill in. Even though some things had died in our absence, the yard looked lush as always, an overgrown paradise of flowers and trees.

There was a lot to accomplish in a short time, so they got right to work. Kjell's seminar went well. Having lived in the

Ivory Coast before, he knew how to relate to the Ivorians, and they loved him. Since he is fluent in French, he gave the seminar in that language for those who could understand it, and Csaba had one of the villagers translate into Bakwé for the rest. Even though he suffered from the intense heat and humidity, Kjell said that this trip was one of the highlights of his life.

Csaba met with the translation team and got a report of what they had been doing in his absence. It was both encouraging and discouraging at the same time, but that was to be expected with him working remotely from the team. The book of Galatians had been completed, and a Bakwé bilingual dictionary had been published. The literacy classes we had started before we left were continuing on in seven villages, and devotions were being led in the classes with readings from 1 John in Bakwé. It was wonderful to see them using the translated Scriptures. Pastor Firmain and Alexis were leading the church in the village, and it had grown since we'd last seen it. A second church had been planted in Oupoyo, a village to the north of ours.

The translation was proceeding at a much slower pace than expected due to illness, computer difficulties, and the unreliable internet connection, but it had not stopped. Csaba and the team discussed ways to increase efficiency and productivity and minimize the interruptions. Csaba wanted to get a better internet connection at the translation office to allow him daily contact with the team. Up to this point, they had only been able to connect using the satellite modem once a week because of the high cost of data transmission.

Csaba and Kjell visited a Togolese man to show their students an example of a successful cottage business. Afterward, they sat down for some refreshments. The Togolese man got up and thanked Csaba for the counsel and help he had given him years before that had saved his marriage from divorce. It was very encouraging for Csaba to come back and see this thriving Christian family.

They also visited Fani, a man from the Senoufo territory in the north of Ivory Coast who grew up in a Muslim family. Fani came to our village because his Muslim uncle who lived there promised him work in his carpentry shop, provided he attend the mosque while he was there. They practiced what is called folk Islam, which is Islam syncretized with traditional African beliefs.

Csaba had hired Fani to do work on our house and talked with him a lot. Through Csaba and other Christians, Fani heard the gospel but thought it was just a cultural thing. He didn't understand that becoming a Christian meant a complete change of heart. Yet there was something in the Christians that he wanted. Fani had a brother who was a Christian, and he had seen his life change. When he saw the same fruit in Csaba's life, he thought it must be more than a cultural thing, since Christians from different cultures, Bakwé and American, seemed to have this fruit.

One day, Csaba drove to San-Pédro with Fani to get supplies. Csaba witnessed to him and answered a lot of his questions. He told him that he could accept Christ right now. He just needed to confess his sins before God and give himself to the Lord by accepting His gift of salvation through Jesus Christ's death on the cross. Fani went to church the next day and said that he wanted to become a Christian. After this, he was baptized and began growing in the Lord. Soon he noticed that he now had that fruit in his life.

But with that joy came hardship. When his uncle found out that Fani had become a Christian, he kicked him out. Fani had to find a new place for his wife, daughter, and newborn baby to live and set up shop in a different part of town. In his first year, his Muslim family up north kept saying, "You don't love us because you don't send your children to be with us." Finally, he gave in and sent his daughter to visit them. She was eight or nine years old at the time. One day while his daughter was up north with his family, Fani was told that she had just dropped dead after walking across the courtyard. To this day, he doesn't know exactly what happened, but he suspects it was foul play in retaliation for his conversion to Christianity.

A month after the daughter's death, their baby died. On hearing this news, Fani's whole Muslim family said that it was because he had become a Christian and Allah was punishing him. Christians prayed for Fani and his wife during this hard time, and they gathered around to encourage him. The couple remained faithful to God despite losing their two children. They had found the truth and were not about to leave it, no matter what happened to them. God gave them two more children after that. Fani had held fast to God through adversity, and it was good for Csaba to see him still going strong after so many years.

Chapter 16
At Home

> Judge not the Lord by feeble sense,
> But trust Him for His grace;
> Behind a frowning providence
> He hides a smiling face. (Cowper)

I WAS THANKFUL FOR OUR WONDERFUL children and for the good people in the church who offered to help while Csaba was away. God answered prayer and sustained my limited strength. I even found a way to sweep our dining room with much less effort. Instead of moving all the chairs to get the broom under the table, I took the leaf blower, opened the French doors to the garden, and cleared the place out in seconds.

The children also kept me amused. Jeremiah took up a new indoor sport of getting around the house without touching the ground. He had amazing agility, so he could make it around the living room, into the kitchen, and through the dining room without coming down once. This required quite a few stretches and rock-climbing techniques. I'm not sure if he can list this as a skill on a job application, but I was impressed nonetheless.

Jeremiah's Spider-Man skills came into play in other ways, too. He had a habit of flipping himself upside down while holding onto the door jamb, causing only his head to poke down from the top of the door. It always freaked me out when I came around a corner and ran into a bodiless, upside-down face grinning at me. He was a kid without a decent tree to climb, so he took to climbing everything else.

Soon Csaba returned from Africa, and we were glad to see him. As usual, he was at work during the days, and the kids were at school, so the house still felt pretty empty, especially since I continued to spend a lot of time down. I needed something to help fill the quiet hours at home. I presented this need to the Lord, and one day I saw an advertisement in the paper for African Grey parrots, the same type we had in the village! I was thrilled at the prospect, but the parrots were expensive and beyond our budget. Yet God had recently blessed Csaba with two speaking engagements that gave him honorariums, so we were able to afford the parrot, and Saki (named for an African chief we knew) came into our lives.

Saki became quite the presence in our household. Instead of silence, we now had a feathered two-year-old who demanded constant attention. I spent months talking to him, saying the same things over and over, but the first word he said was *oink*, followed by *meow*. I wrote my sister, "Well, we're hearing a new animal lately. It's the cat. It's a rather drunk cat with digestive problems, but it's a cat nonetheless, and it's in our living room with the herd of pigs from last week. I wonder what animal will be next?"

Saki went on to mimic goats, owls, doves, dogs, chickens, and roosters. Then he began to pick up other sounds, like the ringtone from our landline. He could do a very convincing ring. After several dashes to grab the ringing phone and finding only the parrot instead, I changed the ringtone. I had to change it three times before I hit on one he couldn't successfully mimic.

The parrot could be a problem when he picked up a new sound. One day, I was talking on the phone with an insurance agent, and I happened to have the parrot on my shoulder. (Note to self: Don't do this again.) As I was waiting for an answer to a question I had asked, my bird took that moment of silence to make a kissing sound, loud and clear. Embarrassed, I explained where that sound had come from, hoping very much that the agent believed me, because Saki had gone silent again. Thankfully, the conversation soon ended. One thing I did know was that the parrot would not be on my shoulder the next time I made a business call.

ATTEMPTING CHURCH (AGAIN)

By 2007, I had been doing church on my mat on the darkened stage for roughly a year. I wanted to try sitting through a whole service again, since the backstage spot was meant to be a temporary solution. The goal was to get back to the banquet, not live in the shadows. One Sunday, I gave it a go.

As I sat in my chair, I looked around the church. The place was filled with a joyful throng, and I felt part of a grand movement marching on to glory. How I had missed being with everyone! The singing was robust, and it brought me up to the heavenlies, or rather it brought heaven down to me. Although the rest of the congregation stood for many of the hymns, I sang sitting down, mouthing the words so I could conserve energy. The sermon was preached with power, and I drank it in like a thirsty traveler at a fresh well. But as the preaching continued, fatigue began to wash over me. It became harder and harder to focus on the sermon. Soon the stream of words became a muddle in my mind, and I concentrated only on staying in the service, nothing more.

When the congregation stood to raise their hands for the closing benediction, I was hunched over in my seat. After the service, Csaba wanted to talk to someone briefly, so he slipped off into the crowd. My kids did the same. I gathered my coat into my lap and sat there. I really couldn't do anything else.

As I waited for Csaba, I became more aware of what was happening around me. The church was a busy place after the service. People ambled by going nowhere and everywhere, bumping into each other and greeting as they went. Children dashed past. Grandmothers bent down to hug their grandkids. Groups of people stood and talked.

It had only been ten minutes since the service had ended, yet my energy loss was severe. I looked around for Csaba, but he was still talking to someone, and I was too weak to go get him. I leaned back in my chair. The noise in the gym became one big confusion, and my brain felt like it was short fusing. Csaba returned, helped me out of my chair, and we walked very slowly to the car.

Once we were back at the house, I lay down and shut my eyes to settle the confusion that was still swirling in my brain. After a bit, a little strength returned, enough to talk, and we discussed ways to handle this problem next time.

Staying through church would continue to prove challenging. Over the years to follow, I kept at it until I could sit through the service a little better. But what was wrong with me? Why was I not any better after several years of resting? Why did it feel like I was carrying that five-hundred-pound backpack all the time? The word *tired* just didn't seem adequate to describe how I felt. It was an incapacitating weakness that affected every area of my body. It put me continuously on a bed of suffering, both physically and emotionally, from which I could not escape.

Chapter 17
June Trip

CSABA WENT TO IVORY COAST AGAIN for three weeks in June 2007. This time, Hans' friend Benjamin went with him to help with certain projects. While they were there, Csaba had the books of Galatians and James checked by a translation consultant. He was pleased to hear from the consultant that the team was doing a good job. After the checking was completed, Csaba worked on the glossary and notes, then helped the team with troubleshooting and planning out the next phase of the translation.

While Csaba was doing this, Benjamin had his own work to do. First, he ran a two-day seminar for the Bakwé on small business practices, using a translator to interpret.

Then he set up a recording studio and trained the Bakwé team on using the new audio gear and software he and Csaba had brought. Benjamin hit it off with the team right away, and Csaba, busy with translation work, could often hear laughing in the next room or singing as Benjamin played his guitar.

Benjamin helped in other areas as well, like setting up a wireless network, which took a full day. When one guy's computer could finally see the wireless internet box in the next room, that person would shout, "My computer wins!" When at last Benjamin got everyone's computer connected, Firmain was so happy that he asked Benjamin what type of meat he could cook for him as a thank you.

On Sunday, they visited the Harrist Church in the village. On Monday, people from that church came to the house to thank Csaba for the money that our church back home had given them to help construct their building. Many people thanked Csaba for what we were doing among the Bakwé and for the Scriptures that had already been translated.

Csaba wrote me about one memorable event. Perez, a member of the translation team, brought an older woman from the northern village of Gblétia who had learned to read. He was proud of her accomplishment and wanted to show Csaba. Perez handed her a primer the team had put together, and she read the first several pages that had pictures with them. Csaba praised her but wondered if she had just memorized the words that went with the pictures. It is hard for adults to learn to read, and we discovered that many of the older Bakwé had simply memorized the primers instead. But then she fumbled in her bag and pulled out a worn copy of the Bakwé Gospel of John. She opened it and began to read fluently. She stopped and explained to Perez how she had read the whole thing up to the point where it talked about Jesus dying. She said the other ethnic groups had their Bibles, but the Bakwé did not yet, but now she could read it in her own language! She said that many Bakwé don't see the importance of reading, so she was on a campaign to tell everyone to learn to read for themselves. Csaba was touched to see someone who'd had no access to God's Word before actually reading it!

Csaba missed us and wrote that it was hard to be in the village without us. There were so many memories of us all around. He knew the pain we felt at being separated from the place and people we loved. "Don't look on the half-empty side of the cup and miss God's best for you, which is what is happening right now," he wrote to me. "His presence is sufficient. 'At His right hand are blessings forevermore.' Remember, the Author is divine. He hasn't finished writing our story yet. I would love for you all to be here with me, but I sure wouldn't want to take the pen out of God's hand. He knows how His story for you will end. I pray that you take joy in being where you are, knowing His presence in dark times like no one else can that hasn't gone through the things you have."

Chapter 18

The Sun Behind the Mist

> His purposes will ripen fast,
> Unfolding every hour;
> The bud may have a bitter taste,
> But sweet will be the flower. (Cowper)

ONE WINTER MORNING IN 2008, CSABA looked out the kitchen window and said, "Come summer, this spot will be a garden of flowers once more. It is hard to believe that there is actual life under that hard earth, but it is there waiting. Spring follows winter, summer follows spring, and God causes resurrection after death."

I always enjoyed the fresh blooms of the garden after months of cold, dreary weather and was thankful that spring kept coming year after year no matter how hard the winter was. I longed to get out into the garden but still couldn't work much, so Jeremiah was enlisted. Watching him digging, readying the garden beds, and planting new bulbs and starts brought me joy and something to look forward to as the garden blossomed into a cascade of color. We had installed a little pond and waterfall next to the back patio, and I loved to sit and listen as it bubbled and tumbled in a never-ending cycle of joy. The garden slowly developed into a colorful paradise, bringing me much pleasure as it reminded me of God's resurrection patterns.

Since I had been cooped up so much over the winter, Csaba started taking me out for short, quiet walks in the countryside or for a little biking. I would coast down a gently-sloping portion of our local bike path while Csaba took the car, parked it at the bottom of the path, and biked up to rejoin me halfway down. His thoughtfulness displayed the unique love of Christ at work in practical ways.

One season blended into the next with my kids busy with school and sports. Andreas was on the high school lacrosse team, and Jeremiah ran cross country.

I was finally able to drive myself around town a little and even walk a bit on my own for exercise, though not every day or very far. I was invited to join a group of women who regularly got together to walk for exercise along a pleasant road out of town. I was happy for the chance, even though we all knew ahead of time that I would not be able to keep up with them for long and would have to head back by myself. Regardless, I decided it would be wonderful to take part for however long I could.

On the day of the first walk, we headed out at a relaxed pace, breaking off into little groups as we went. As we walked, warm conversation flew around me as people chatted happily. Although I remained silent to conserve my energy, I really enjoyed being with them.

Unfortunately, we had hardly gone more than a hundred yards when my breathing became labored, and I realized that I would not last long. After another hundred yards, my energy was finished. After stopping for a while to catch my breath, I turned back toward the cars.

As I hauled myself back to the starting point, I was met with comparative stillness—just the wind blowing softly in the grass by the empty road. The silence and emptiness seemed to represent my life now. Shuffling back at a ridiculously slow pace, I could hear the trickle of water in the ditch, which I hadn't noticed before. The sun beat down on the fields, and an occasional bird flew by. Other than these things, it was just me, the road, and the emptiness of the countryside.

Step followed heavy step. Thought followed weary thought—my body telling me to stop, that it was done for the day, or was it done for the week? I wouldn't know until I got back home and could assess the damage I had just done. With waves of fatigue washing over me, I got in my car to drive back home while I still could. I realized I was not strong enough yet to take part in a group.

I took my walks alone in a different place closer to home and at a slower pace. One day, God used an incident to teach me something. I was out on a country road by the University of Idaho sheep barn on a foggy day. The visibility was limited due to a dark blanket of mist that enveloped the landscape, weighing it down. As I trudged along in the quiet of that somber day, the sheep formed hazy shapes out in the fields. Beyond them were outlines of buildings and farm equipment resting in the shadows, seemingly asleep. The leaves dripped softly, letting go of the moisture that was accumulating on their wet surfaces. All was a damp silence.

Then something broke the reverie of the morning. From behind me, somewhere in the shadows of the mist, I heard warm laughter. This time, I just wanted to avoid people because being left behind on a walk reminded me of how shut out of the entire life of fellowship I was.

I made a quick decision and took a side road, thinking whoever was behind me would take the main one. I plunged into the mist, musing that I could handle things better if I didn't have to see what I was missing in life. I trudged very slowly up a hill flanked by the shady shapes of trees, a rusty fence, and the dripping grass beside me.

But God had other plans. The laughter didn't fade like I wanted; it remained constant. Puzzled, I looked back, but couldn't see anyone, so I went on with my plodding pace.

Surprisingly, the bubble of fellowship got louder, so I looked back again, and this time saw blurry shapes coming my way. The shapes grew larger and clearer until a voice greeted me. I turned around and realized it was someone I knew, so I greeted them back. They stayed and chatted with me for a minute, and in that minute I was enveloped in the warmth of their fellowship. I had been trying to avoid it, but here it was blessing me after all. Soon they gave their parting goodbyes and set out at a hearty pace up the hill. As they went, their shapes became blurred by the hazy surroundings, then were engulfed in the mist until I could see them no more. But through gray fog I could still hear their happy chatter lingering on until the bubble of warmth went up over the hill and faded away completely.

I turned to go back down the hill in the direction I had come, since my strength would allow no more. By now, the mist was icy cold. The silence closed in again, and I was left alone with my thoughts. How could it be so cold when it wasn't really cold? Silent world, dripping mist, tears flowing down my cheeks—I was derailed again. When would I learn to handle isolation? Does it come in time? Or would it always be this way? Sometimes it is not what you never had but what you once had, then lost, that hurts the most.

When I got home, I told Csaba how I felt so bone-chillingly alone. Csaba listened sympathetically, then reminded me, "But you weren't alone. You were walking with God. Where God is, there is always light and warmth and fellowship. You just have to have eyes to see it and access it in a different way."

I had almost forgotten this most important fellowship—one that can never be taken away. I thanked God for His presence and for my husband's wisdom which helped me to see the sun behind the mist. The warm, joyful sun of God's presence can shine through even the darkest, coldest fog. You just have to have eyes to see it.

"For the LORD God is a sun and shield; the Lord will give grace and glory; no good thing will He withhold from those who walk uprightly" (Psalm 84:11).

Somewhere along the line, my friend Brenda came to help. She has a personal ministry to those who are hurting. I don't know exactly when I got on her radar, but I did, and she asked what she could do for me. I said I'd love it if she could walk with me at my pace. So we walked together slowly a handful of times over the next few months whenever I was up for it, which was sporadic. It was delightful to be with her. God had arranged this time in His mercy and kindness for me, His hurting child, because He understood my need.

Something else Csaba said concerning isolation was profoundly helpful to me during this time. "Relationships are like corks drifting slowly along a wide river. Sometimes the corks will be together, and sometimes they will drift apart with the current and form other groupings. But according to the nature of streams and currents, the corks will sometimes come together again. It is a dynamic process, not a static one."

God is the one who controls the currents. He moves people around for His own purposes, and we need to be faithful with what God has given us and flow in the direction He chooses, even if it takes us away from what we knew before. If we find ourselves alone for a while on a stretch of stream, it won't be forever. Our goal is not to stay in the same place on the stream but to be faithful to where God moves us. If we try to keep everything the same when the current is moving us on, then we will be unable to experience all the *good* things God wants to accomplish in and through us. Our goal as Christians is not changelessness, but faithfulness where God puts us, even if it is in an eddy off to the side for a time.

Chapter 19
A New Old Car

>   Blind unbelief is sure to err
>   And scan His work in vain;
>   God is His own interpreter,
>   And He will make it plain. (Cowper)

SINCE OUR RETURN TO IDAHO, WE HAD been driving a used car, one that had been donated to our mission and was given to us. It worked, but with a few difficulties. With some trouble, we had managed to navigate its eccentricities for a few years, and mostly were just happy that we had transportation.

Then God mercifully put it upon the hearts of a dear couple in our church to get us another car. Csaba and I were both astounded when we heard the news.

That week, I had been having a series of rough days that had affected me both physically and emotionally. I had to keep fighting to come back up out of discouragement. Before Sunday, I became disheartened in a deeper way. I wasn't getting victory over it like I usually did, even after confessing being discouraged. I needed to get back into the battle but was having a hard time doing it.

During times like this, I knew that God would reach down and encourage me in some way. He always did. These moments were like a divine parting of the clouds, as if God was saying, "I know it's been hard. I love you, and everything will be alright. Here's your sword, and here's your shield. Come now, let's get up and keep fighting." Then I would get a grip on my emotions and move on with renewed hope.

At church, as I was sitting down resting before the service started, Csaba said, "I wanted to let you know that so-and-so wants to give us a car."

I was overwhelmed. "You're kidding! Why would they want to do that? I mean, we have a car—sort of."

Csaba responded, "Yes, but he said it was nonnegotiable and to come along quietly, if you please."

I remember thinking, "I don't deserve this. I really don't." Then I felt that divine presence saying, "I love you." There it was again, a lavish gift I did not deserve, and God was offering it—freely. It was the exact encouragement I had been needing, and I felt His presence so close that I started to cry silent happy tears while I sat there in church. I tried not to think about it, to stop the tears, but words in the Psalm singing and verses in the Bible reading kept leaping out at me, speaking directly to my heart and encouraging me, which made me cry more. Since I didn't want to make a scene, when the prayer time came and everyone's eyes were closed, I slipped out of my seat and went outside to let the emotion of thankfulness out. God had sent the encouragement I needed through that human channel.

JEREMIAH RUNNING

One recurrent blessing from God during those years of down time was Jeremiah's running. He was often the front runner for his high school team during his freshman year. He ran with a fluidness that was a joy to watch. When I was able, I went to his cross-country meets in the fall and track meets in the spring, sitting on my camp stool on the sidelines to watch him race. Being part of his sport brought me out of my world of sickness and gave me something (and someone else) to be excited about and concentrate on.

Csaba and I were proud of Jeremiah's determination and hard work in the sport. The summer after his freshman year, he trained harder and ended up with a stress fracture that removed him for the entire cross-country season his sophomore year. His leg wasn't healed enough for him to run track in the spring, either, which meant he was out of sports for the full year. That was a test for his character. It's fun to be in front leading the pack, but the real challenge for a boy is seeing how he handles being knocked down and having to watch those who used to be behind him take his place.

Jeremiah was determined not to let being on the sidelines get him down. At each track meet, he set up the tent beforehand and took it down again at the end, encouraged the other runners before their races, and cheered them on while they competed. He did it without complaining, even though he was longing to get back out there with them. He continued to watch from the sidelines the entire track season while encouraging, helping, and supporting the others on the team.

At the track awards banquet, Jeremiah knew he would not get anything. He cheered for his teammates as they went forward to receive their awards. At the end, the coach announced, "We have one more award. It is the highest award you can receive at this school in any sport. It is the Knight's Award, and it is given to the athlete who best exemplifies the attitude, work ethic, and sacrifice that reflects a Christian athlete. This award goes to Jeremiah Leidenfrost."

We were so proud of him. He did not come in first in any race, but he proved his ability to hold up under hardship, to not give in to trying circumstances, and instead to stand strong and serve others, which to us and to God are much more valuable achievements.

Jeremiah went on to run again for the next two years. He was a good solid runner, though no longer a front runner. No matter—Jeremiah was a champion in our eyes.

ccc

I was so proud of Jeremiah for holding up under hard trials and not giving in to circumstances, but at the same time I was finding it a constant challenge to do this myself. I was in the major leagues with my ongoing ordeal, and I was not finding it easy, even after all my training in the minor leagues.

At some point, I began to question God about the length and severity of the trial He had given me. I even went through the book of Job and highlighted all the verses where I felt the same way Job did. The answer that was impressed upon me in my questioning was always, "Wait. Trust Me."

But my trial didn't make sense, nor did there seem an end in sight. Therefore, it was crucial for me to return to *what I knew to be true* and stand there—on God's character and His promises. It was safe there. Yes, God was extremely hard on Job, and Job wanted to know why, but in the end, God never gave him a direct answer. He only said in so many chapters, "Look at who I am; that is enough for you."

Therefore, if I know that God is all-powerful, all-knowing, and all-good, then I can be assured that His power in my life will be used for ultimate good. When I know and remember that He loves me, I don't need to fear. When I look to Him in faith, I can believe that He will work it all out. I don't need to know *how*. I don't need to know *when*. All I need to know is that God knows exactly what He is doing in my life.

In studying the book of Job, I could see as a reader what Job couldn't see as the main character in his own story: that God meant his trial for a blessing. This blessing was not only for Job, but for the whole world who would read about his hardships in the Bible. Now, thousands of years later, I am helped by it. But at the time, Job couldn't understand. In the thick of it, he was convinced that God was being way too hard on him. But in the end, Job saw God's justice and faithfulness throughout it all.

Chapter 20

The Locked Door

> There is a way of setting the life of holiness before the believer so as to make them think that it is a mountain that must be climbed. But actually, the mountain of God's foreordaining grace is behind us, and the river runs down it, carrying us to His great sea of kindness. The effort we exert is given its force because of what lies behind. Through this effort we obtain what lies ahead of us, but we must never forget that it is the river that carries us. And the troubles we encounter are nothing but patches of white water. (Douglas Wilson)

MOSCOW, 2009

It had been four years since our return to Idaho, and my quest to reenter life hadn't gotten very far. Large groups were still too difficult for me to handle, especially in the evenings when I was at my lowest. I wanted to keep trying, but often when I did, the life of fellowship continued to elude me. I didn't want to stay on the sidelines for the rest of my life.

So we tried a new strategy. When I felt up to accepting an invitation for a gathering, we instituted a plan for conserving my energy: we would arrive late, then have me sit down right after entering. Csaba would be ready to head out if I felt I was going under. With these new safeguards in place, I could last a little bit longer than usual.

As Csaba talked to the people in the air above me at a party or other gathering, I would usually sit on the side and observe. Watching the pockets of people talking and fellowshipping around me, a twang of longing would often hit me. I had the *time* for relationships, but not the energy. To have a conversation, you must engage in it. But I only had enough strength to sit and watch. What a dilemma! On top of that, because I usually sat in a quiet place on the sidelines, I was continually (and inadvertently) giving off social cues that I wanted to be left alone. It was maddening. I felt like an emaciated child pressing its nose on the window of a candy shop and looking in while all the other children were inside indulging in the delights it offered. The irony was that even if people wandered over to me to talk (which was a delight), I wouldn't be able to respond much. The energy of talking was still very difficult for me, which often left the conversation fairly one-sided.

When my strength gave way, and the room became a blur of confusion, Csaba would help me to the car, where the quiet drive home could soothe my spinning head, and the confusion would start to abate. After we got home, and I had rested a bit, Csaba would faithfully remind me to look up to Christ in all things.

I looked back on such events with a mixture of both pleasure and pain: pleasure because I had been there and pain because I really had not. Even though friends came to visit or to offer a "cup of cold water" through practical help or encouragement in various ways, I was still a functional shut-in. I was hungry for life. I missed people. I missed taking part in conversations and contributing something worthwhile. I missed going out for coffee or being at an event with friends and enjoying fellowship and laughter. I missed having people over and serving them, then cleaning up afterwards and getting my hands dirty doing it. I missed going to Christmas parties, making cookies, and shopping for something fun to give someone. I missed talking with people after church and standing up while doing it.

It wasn't just fellowship I was missing. I missed the *freedom* you have when you are healthy. I missed taking long hikes, going around the next bend and the next, just to see where they went. I missed working in my garden, feeling the earth between my fingers, and digging new garden beds all by myself. I missed brisk walks in the summer sun, feeling my lungs and legs working hard and my body sweating. I missed going wherever I wanted, and as fast and far as I wanted.

I was tired of lying down, feeling awful, and getting up and feeling awful when I did that, too. I wandered aimlessly about the house just to relieve the suffering of being down, determined to do something, *anything*, rather than lie in bed endlessly, feeling neither alive nor dead.

On top of all this, a subtle grief over the loss of Africa continued to grip my heart. In my dismal state, at one particular moment when I was badly in need of encouragement, I felt the clouds part and God's presence come down to touch His child, just to say how much He loved me still. God saw the pain, the loneliness, the need, and was telling me that *I was not forgotten*. It was too easy to focus on my troubles. I needed to remember that God's love is stronger, more real, than the pain I was suffering at that moment. Was I going to focus on His love, or on the pain?

The apostle Paul had to learn contentment in all the various hard situations he found himself in, whether full or hungry, abounding or suffering need. He was able do it through the strength that Christ gave each day. "Not that I speak in regard to need, for I have learned in whatever state I am, to be content: I know how to be abased, and I

THE LOCKED DOOR

know how to abound. Everywhere and in all things I have learned both to be full and to be hungry, both to abound and to suffer need. I can do all things through Christ who strengthens me" (Phil. 4:11–13).

Could I have this contentment as well? I certainly wanted it. Then at church one Sunday, our assistant pastor gave a homily that really hit home.

> To know Christ is to be enrolled in the school of contentment. It means learning to be content in whatever state you are in. Contentment is not stoicism. It does not mean having no feelings. No, contentment means knowing Christ, resting in Christ, being so completely sure of the goodness and love of Christ, that you rest assured that your circumstances are serving Christ's purposes perfectly.
>
> If Christ is your Savior, then He is saving you to the uttermost. He is saving you through the circumstances of your life. Sometimes life hurts, sometimes it's scary, but if you know Christ, you know that He holds all things together in His infinite wisdom for His glory and your good.
>
> So, what is God doing with your life? He is doing exactly what it takes to make you into the image of Christ. He is infinite, and this means that He has infinite care for every detail. And so, your task is to trust Him. And Paul says this means rejoicing

always and in all things. He is preparing you for infinite joy. And He is doing exactly what it takes to get you there.[1]

---

[1]. Toby Sumpter, "Even All the Scaffolding Serves Him," *Having Two Legs* (blog), September 15, 2018, https://tobyjsumpter.com/even-all-the-scaffolding-serves-him.

Chapter 21

The Answer

> The day is Yours, the night also is Yours. (Ps. 74:16a)

"DO YOU EVER THINK ABOUT DYING?" Meredith asked me one day.

I said, "Yes. If the doctor told me that I had incurable cancer, I think I might actually be relieved that my suffering would be coming to an end."

I didn't really want to leave this earth. I just wanted *relief*. Even after years of fatigue with not much change and no diagnosis, I still had a feeling that something was drastically wrong underneath it all. Throughout this time, various suggestions for this or that alternative remedy had been presented to us by well-meaning people. Normally they were very gracious and went through Csaba, both of which we appreciated. I hardly had the capacity to decide which breakfast cereal to eat, let alone sort through different suggestions for medical treatment. We kept in mind the advice our missionary doctor had given us that some alternative treatments can be harmful. Yet some of them might be helpful, so Csaba screened them and presented each one to the Lord.

There were still times when I had to deal with the people who presented the remedies. One day, a concoction was dropped off at the house with a note saying that it would cure me. I told Csaba, who looked at the ingredients and decided it would be best not to use it, however miraculous it might prove to be. Soon after, the giver called to make sure I had received her cure and was indeed using it. When I replied that I was not, an ordeal began.

I hardly had energy for a normal conversation, let alone wrestling her down to accepting the reality that we had decided not to take it. She verged on hysterical as she told me the virtues of this wonder drug and why it would save me and our ministry. After a ten-minute *ode to a drug* routine, I felt she was getting close to weeping, when my brain began to short-fuse. I needed to lie down, so while she continued to talk, I said that I was going to leave now, thank you, and goodbye. Then I hung up. I don't know how long she kept going before she realized she had no audience.

All of the alternative-remedy suggestions were looked into and ultimately rejected. I was quite willing to try something new since my life was so miserable as it was, but I was also so weak that I couldn't afford to get worse through a false turn. Csaba didn't have the peace to go ahead with any of the suggested home remedies, so we didn't try them. I appreciated his decision-making. It was a good thing we didn't try them, because in the end none of those things would have worked, and some could have made me worse.

Through it all, we kept looking to the Lord for wisdom. He knew exactly what was wrong with me, and He knew the cure. If we looked to Him, He would guide us. If I was to be healed, we wanted it to come through Him first, and not from us grabbing frantically at every shiny thing that presented itself as the way out.

Sleep had been hard for years. In fact, I had trouble falling asleep. When I relaxed and started to slip through the door of slumber, a loud noise would jerk me back to wakefulness. When that happened, I checked my breathing to be sure nothing was obstructing my airway. I wasn't sure what was making the noise. When repeated attempts didn't produce sleep, I would take part of a sleeping pill to kick me over the initial barrier. After I managed to fall asleep, I would keep waking up throughout the night. I didn't sleep deeply—ever. I also rarely dreamed.

I felt uneasy about the nights. I remember being distressed about it and telling Csaba. He thought it was just anxiety, so he told me to give the night to God, then rest in Him. Since being anxious about sleeping was not going to help me sleep, I did just that: I asked God to guard me, since once I went through the door of sleep, I had no control over what happened to me.

Every morning, I awoke feeling like I had been in a battle, yet I had no idea what the battle was. All that I knew was that I needed the day to recover from the night. By the end of the day, I was so tired that I needed the night to recover from the day—but that was when I was going back to battle again.

I asked God to protect me and control what I could not. God put Himself between me and the unseen abyss that was right next to me all those years. Every night, as I drifted off into the unknown, God was asking me not to be anxious, and to *trust Him*.

> O LORD my God, I cried out to You,
> And You healed me.
> O LORD, You brought my soul up from the grave;
> You have kept me alive, that I should not go down
>   to the pit. (Ps. 30:2–3)

This trial had been a very long haul, but God had already decided the beginning, the duration, and the end of it. One day, He opened the prison doors.

In July 2010, we went camping. I loved camping but hadn't been strong enough to do it in years. Since it seemed I was not likely to ever get better, we decided to make it work anyhow. We went car camping at a spot overlooking a mountain lake near the Idaho-Montana border. The elevation at the campground was 7,000 feet, meaning the air was much thinner than we were used to.

We set up our tents and settled in for the evening. That night, I dreamed that I was being held under water for a long time. I kept trying to reach the surface to take a breath but couldn't. Finally, when my lungs could take it no more, I shot up from my sleeping bag gasping for breath. Slowly the panic of almost drowning subsided, and I realized that I had had a nightmare and should just go back to sleep. But to what—more nightmare? more danger? I didn't know, so I asked God to be with my every breath, a request that had become my regular nighttime prayer.

The next morning, Noai told us that someone had been repeatedly gasping for breath and choking throughout the night.

I looked at her in dead earnestness. "This is *really* important: tonight, find out who it is."

That night, Noai discovered that it was me. In the morning, she informed us. "Oh Mom," she cried, "it was so scary hearing you gasp for breath all night long." That was all the evidence we needed.

I told John Grauke, our friend and family doctor, and he ordered a sleep study. As I waited for it to be scheduled, I hoped that this would be the key to let me out. The night of the study, Csaba and I went to the local hospital's sleep lab. The technician was a man whose specialty was sleep studies, so his days and nights were switched. As he stuck adhesive electrodes here and there on my skin and hooked them up to various wires, he chatted with Csaba as if it was the middle of the day. I was groggy and wanted to wind down, but it was hard with all the energetic conversation around me. I interrupted to ask him what the solution would be if I had sleep apnea, and he told me that for mild apnea I could have a mouth guard to keep my airway open. For moderate to severe apnea, I would need a CPAP machine, but he didn't think I would be that bad and told me not to worry about it.

After I was wired up, I climbed into the bed in the sleep study suite, and Csaba lay down on a cot to the side.

In the morning, the technician came into the room wide-eyed. "You are one of the *worst* cases of sleep apnea I have ever seen. Bad, real bad!" He had been afraid that I was going to die during the night; it was all he could do to keep from rushing into the room and waking me up. He said that I'd have to wait for the doctor to hear the specific results, but I had sleep apnea, alright.[1]

At our follow-up appointment with Dr. Grauke, he too had the same look of astonishment as the technician. He

---

1. The high-altitude campground was instrumental in us discovering this; the lack of oxygen in the air made my sleep apnea worse, and I gasped for breath loudly enough for others to notice.

said that I had stopped breathing for various lengths of time *over eighty times an hour*, which explained my nightmare about being held under water. He explained that since my body had to keep waking me up to breathe, I was going into REM sleep only 1 percent of the night. REM, which stands for rapid eye movement, is the stage of the sleep cycle where the brain gets rejuvenated, and typically makes up about 20 to 30 percent of sleep time. Lack of brain-repairing sleep combined with nightly oxygen deprivation had altered my body's systems, emotions, and mind, causing the fatigue, fuzzy thinking, and low spirits that had plagued me for years.

The treatment for this was a CPAP machine. The CPAP (continuous positive airway pressure) machine blows a continuous stream of air into the upper respiratory passage, forcing the airway to stay open. Dr. Grauke set me up for a second sleep study to calibrate a machine for me.

I badly wanted to have that machine right away, but I had to wait for the study and hope my body wouldn't give out in the meantime. The nights that followed were torture. I was feeling poorly, and now I knew why. It was scary to go back into the battle of the night knowing it was truly a battle. Again, we entrusted each night to God and let it go. God is the God of the night as well as the day, and He hadn't changed just because I now knew what was going on.

When we arrived at the sleep clinic for the second study, I was prepared for the rousing conversation from our exuberant technician. This time, the topic was how serious sleep apnea could be and how it affected every area of the body.

I was fitted with a mask and went to sleep. The technician consulted the readouts and adjusted the pressure on the CPAP during the night to stop the apnea. I slept well, better than I had in a long, long time. In the morning, I felt refreshingly different, like someone had thrown open a window in a stuffy room and let in a fresh breeze. I called Csaba, who had gone home to sleep this time. "Something's different! I feel alive again!" The well of my strength had been stopped up for so long, but now the energy was flowing in me once more.

Csaba met me at the hospital for breakfast, and we rejoiced together, celebrating the dawning of a new day after so many years of hard night. I was issued my own CPAP machine, and what happened next was something on the level of miraculous. Whole systems in my body, as well as emotions, outlook, and mental capacity, snapped back into place in quick succession.

In the first few days after getting the machine, I just wanted to move. In fact, I didn't want to *stop* moving! The first day, I cleaned the house even though it wasn't dirty—simply because I could. I kept cleaning and cleaning in wild abandon, and when I looked at the clock it was two hours past noon!

Each morning, I woke up to a new day with something else clicking back on that had been *off* before. My blood sugar levels stayed normal instead of running either too high or too low. My blood pressure went back down into the normal range. My heart, no longer desperately trying to get oxygen, slowed to a normal pace. My skin color changed back to a healthy pink. My mind cleared, and I could think straight again. My brain no longer went into overload in crowds. Almost overnight, my emotions soared back to normal—or past normal. In fact, they ran high, and I started to sing around the house.

The unsettled feeling of being in a battle was gone. I felt a sense of acute wonder at the changes within me. I was a blind person who could suddenly see. I thought, "Wow, this must be what it's like to die and wake up in heaven!"

I was thankful to God for carrying me through the whole trial. He had never forsaken me, because His mercy is everlasting.

I was very thankful to my family who had been with me every step, helping to carry the burden when I could not on my own. I was thankful to Noai, who had taken over my job when I was down and become the best cook ever. I was thankful to our boys who had pitched in without complaining, and I was thankful for Meredith who had gone the second mile in Christlike fashion.

But I was most thankful to Csaba, who had been absolutely incredible, leading me on to Christ every step of the way, sacrificing himself to help carry the very heavy load I was under. He was my personal counselor, support, encouragement, protection, and help, a daily example of the love of Christ in action.

Chapter 22
Reflections on Suffering

> For the creation was subjected to futility, not willingly, but because of Him who subjected it in hope. (Rom. 8:20)

NOW THAT I WAS WELL, I HAD TO DEAL with the inevitable question: Why did I have to suffer so severely for so long when the answer was right at my fingertips? If I had known it was sleep apnea, much suffering could have been avoided.

But there are no *might-have-been*s with God. This was His plan from the beginning. Nothing is a mistake. All is meant to further His purposes. God intends to bring good through suffering. He means it not only for the good of our own souls but for the good of others. God is causing His kingdom to spread throughout the whole earth, and our trials are part of the process.

There are two parts to every trial: the trial itself, and how we deal with it emotionally. How we view hardships really matters. We can see our situation as hopeless and despair, or we can view it with hope and rejoice. We can either see God as being for us, or against us. We can say that the trial was meant for a blessing, or that it was a horrible mistake. The view we take will either lighten our load or make it more than we can bear.

Through suffering and trials, we get more of God. When we don't have any strength of our own, we get to experience *His* strength and learn how to rely on it. We get to know what it is like to be held by the Almighty. We get to know what it is like to be ministered to by the Lord of heaven and earth. Our eyes are opened to what really matters as His lovingkindness and presence become more real to us than ever before. Through suffering, we are prepared for the glory to come as Christ is formed in us. "For our light affliction, which is but for a moment, is working for us a far more exceeding and eternal weight of glory" (2 Cor. 4:17).

The lessons that God taught me in the aftermath of this trial were significant. Some of the harder aspects for me had been losing my sense of identity and being cut off from the life of the living through the isolation my fatigue required.

The ways I had tried to explain my world to myself showed that I was seeing the situation through my own eyes, not through God's. God's work in me through this time helped me see things from a different perspective.

It is easy to connect our identity to what we do and how we interact with those around us. Having these things taken away forces us to look up to Christ, where our true identity lies. If we try to find our identity in our accomplishments and our relationships, we can feel lost when those are taken away. There is *freedom* in knowing that we only have true value and purpose because of Christ. All else is secondary.

The isolation had also affected my sense of belonging. But feelings of isolation and loneliness are normal for mankind. We long for something more, for a deeper fulfillment than we can ever find in relationships here on earth. God has graciously given us a taste of that fulfillment now through the people around us, but the full reality is yet to come. If God puts us in a situation where we are more isolated for a time, it only forces us to look up to where we should have been looking all along—to the satisfaction that can only be found in Christ. Christ alone can satisfy our deepest needs. Our earthly relationships are gifts from God but are not meant to replace our need for Him. God often uses other people to meet our needs in wonderful ways, but if we look to people for help first, they will always let us down in the deepest sense, because they are not divine. If we look to the Lord first, He will always fill us.

We can drink deeply of Christ's well for any need no matter what desert He puts us in. What we are searching for will only be fully realized in heaven; but we have Christ as our guarantee of the fulfillment to come. What we need to remember now is that the living waters of His richness will never stop flowing in our souls, no matter what our situation. God gives us neediness here on earth to cause us to yearn for more of Him. We hunger for the time when we will be completely inundated with His fullness and glory for all eternity. "And let him who thirsts come. Whoever desires, let him take the water of life freely" (Rev. 22:17).

I previously used an analogy of a backpacker to describe how I was feeling. I was entering a banquet in a palace after a long trek in the wilderness. The analogy ended with my human perspective of being shut out. But was that reality?

The story ended with me in a dark, bare room, looking longingly up at the lights of the grand palace and the joy and laughter of a party I couldn't join. But let me finish the story now from a different perspective.

> I was looking out the window, feeling cut off, when I turned around and saw behind me a light coming from another room. I walked into this room and found a table. On it was a white tablecloth and a lantern that glowed softly. Beside the lantern was wine and bread. But the light that had drawn me to this room was not coming from the lantern, but

from behind it where there stood "one like the Son of Man, [whose] countenance was like the sun shining in its strength" (Rev. 1:13, 16). He was beckoning me to come, welcoming me to eat my fill of the living food that would never run out.

Then, from the far corner of the room, another light caught my eye. I looked and saw a door with a crack in it which poured forth a brilliant light, piercingly strong. I walked closer and looked through the opening. Behind the door was a much larger party than the one in the banquet hall, a joyful throng praising the Lord through the most glorious song I had ever heard. As they sang, they looked down to earth and cheered on the saints there to keep pressing forward, standing fast in Christ, and prayed that we would join them soon.

The smaller party I had left in the banquet hall was only a shadow of the much larger, realer one that awaits us in heaven. In Christ, I was already connected to the grander party, even though I couldn't attend the smaller one during my suffering here on earth.

In the truest sense, the reality of being shut out is reserved only for those who are without Christ. They are kept outside in an eternal, empty darkness. In contrast, those who are Christ's are already inside and guests at that grander party, tasting its delights. "My Father gives you the true bread from heaven. For the bread of God is He who comes down from heaven and gives life to the world" (John 6:32–33). In Christ, we are *wanted*, *loved*, and *accepted* at that deep level we all so desperately need.

In my suffering, it was as if God had taken a hot branding iron and burned His mark deep into my soul. The process was one I will never forget, not only because of the pain, but because of what happened after. Like a branding iron, the suffering left an identifiable mark of ownership on me. In the soil of my soul, plants started to grow, then bloom—not in spite of the burning, but *because* of it. If I try to look at that mark now, I can only see a garden in its place, overflowing with flowers. Even if at times I remember the pain of getting it, the memory only drives me more to bring help to others, so that they might also see the hand of the Master Gardener in their lives. In His hands, no trial is ever wasted.

Chapter 23

Don't Waste Your Trials

> This is My commandment, that you love one another as I have loved you. (John 15:12)

NOW THAT I WAS BETTER, I COULD TAKE part in church life again, for real. Our church is a particularly joyful one, a thriving congregation rich in fellowship. Our pastor describes the people as "extraordinarily generous, hardworking, diligent, doctrinally sound, hospitable, and particularly devout." He also said, "We want to create a place to fit in. When there is someone left out, it is a problem to be solved."[1]

1. Douglas Wilson, "State of the Church 2017" (Sermon, Christ Church, Moscow, ID, January 1, 2017).

I wanted to do this. Now that I was strong enough, I wanted to jump in and help meet the needs of the suffering. I wanted to give them a place to come for prayer and encouragement. I didn't want to waste any of the long trial I had just gone through or the lessons I had learned. So I started a small ladies' prayer group with a few of my old friends. We call ourselves the Women of Hope. We are active in praying for each other and in reaching out to encourage others. This group of ladies has done some pretty heavy lifting in prayer and action when it comes to helping women through tough and prolonged trials. They are remarkable in their love for the saints.

I also set up a second prayer group (a much larger one) for the church called Don't Waste Your Trials. It is composed of a core of leaders who are active in reaching out to the suffering women in the church who are dealing with adversities and in need of extra prayer and support, and those who are interested in praying regularly for them. Many of the members have been through their own trials and want to help others in turn. This group operates as an active outreach whose aim is to walk alongside people who are going through trials as we pray with them in confident hope and thankfulness to a great God who answers prayer.

The women in both groups are warriors in caring for the hurting and an active means of building up our local body of Christ. They have prayed each other through many challenges and seen many answers to those prayers. They support and encourage each other through tough times by many different means—visits, gifts, flowers, meals, cards of encouragement. It is such a joy to watch these women in action with their leadership, compassion, creativity, and deep desire to help wherever they can. As we learn together about God's faithfulness through our own trials, we see the waters of blessing from these trials flow through the entire church body, healing and helping as they go.

Here are a couple messages from families who have been ministered to by the church community (including the Don't Waste Your Trials group):

> As much as this all is incredibly hard, there is a part of the body of Christ that we would never have known apart from this trial with our daughter[2]; we would never have known the incredible experience of really being cared for by the body of Christ. There is nothing like it. Thank you all so much for your kindness and generosity.
>
> There have been so many who have stood close by through all of this, continuing to check in on us...letting us know that we are being prayed for. So many people thinking of us, praying for us, emailing us, sending us cards, all giving strength and encouragement as our family worked to find

---
2. A child with a rare but serious disorder.

our footing. We could not have asked for a more loving community to walk through the valley of death than this one. What a privilege it is to have the fellowship of the saints.[3]

If I could describe one scene that sums up the blessing of a church loving its members, it would be what happened when Eileen, the beloved wife of our assistant pastor Mike Lawyer, was dying of cancer. When she became too weak to come to church, the congregation brought church to her on Sunday afternoons, filling their entire yard, spilling out into the street, singing hymns and psalms of praise. Before Mike passed away from cancer himself a few years later, the people of the church were back out on his lawn singing hymns once more, lifting him up to glory.

---

3. This family lost a baby at birth.

Chapter 24

Saying Goodbye

> Surely He has borne our griefs and carried our sorrows. (Isa. 53:4)

SINCE THE IVORY COAST HAD SETTLED down after the war, Csaba took a trip back in June 2012 to have the translation of Acts checked by a consultant while he and Alexis were busy drafting 1 Corinthians.

Meanwhile, I was doing great on the CPAP and wasn't suffering anymore. I thanked God for the machine that had given me lots of energy again. Now that I could think and process things better, I revisited my lack of closure on our life overseas. The hole left in my heart made it difficult to move on. I hadn't had the ability to deal with the grief I felt when we'd left Africa six years earlier, so I had blocked it out. It was the only way I had of handling a difficult situation in my weakened state—but hard memories have a way of popping back up if you don't deal with them.

Now that I was healed and had the strength to deal with this wound, God took off the Band-Aid of my blocking it out and began to deal with the injury underneath in an unexpected way. He took me back in a vision (perhaps you could call it an "awake dream," for I was not asleep) to say goodbye to the past.

I was lying on my bed unable to fall asleep, and my mind wandered. Presently, I was back in Africa again. Even though my eyes were open, they did not see my darkened bedroom in Idaho but apartment 15 in the Abidjan administration center, the place we had always stayed when visiting the city. I found myself standing on the spot where the living room and kitchen met, in front of the half wall that divided the two.

As I stood there, I saw through what seemed like a haze the apartment as we had known it years before. There were the stained walls and the wooden furniture with the faded cloth cushions. There was the single light bulb hanging down from the ceiling and shining through its wicker basket (in reality, long since replaced by a ceiling fan). The glass windowpanes spanning the far wall were framed by curtains of African cloth. Outside, children were playing soccer—mostly African children, but there were white children there, too, all dirty and sweaty with the joy of the game. The coconut trees in the background stood tall against the apartments on the far side of the center.

I turned and looked back into the boys' bedroom. There was the old wooden bunk bed that the kids piled their toys on and the two twin beds outlined with mosquito nets. I could almost hear the rusty fan blades click as they turned. The shelf under the window was piled with stacks of our kids' clothes.

I turned back to the kitchen. In front of me by the wall were the school trunks with their books and papers. When did I last do school? What books had we been reading when we were here? I had forgotten, yet I could see that they were sitting right there in front of me, stacks of books without titles.

On the kitchen table, cardboard boxes sat filled with food from a long-gone supermarket. What were in those boxes? Some special cookies? Or was it Brie cheese? The number of them told me that we must have arrived the day before. The old rickety fridge with its familiar rust spots made a loud humming sound followed by a clank as the compressor started up.

A child entered the room and walked past me. He was about ten years old and had a paper airplane in his hand. Who was that? Oh, it was Hans, the way he used to look when he was much younger, the way I had remembered him in Africa when I wrote the stories in my other books.

Then I saw Noai with her white-blonde, wind-whipped hair. She was clutching dried bits of nature in her hand—perhaps some plants she had found around the center? I wondered if she had lost her flip flops again.

I looked down and saw Jeremiah at my feet. When did he come in, or had he been there the whole time? When had he become so small again? He was just a little guy, hardly more than a toddler, tanned with the sun, and with stains all over his shirt.

Where was Andreas? He was my active one and was probably part of the soccer game out in the yard.

The sounds became more real, as if someone had turned up the volume. I heard the rattle of the palm trees outside the window and the voices of people talking down in the lobby. The center must have been filled with families, because I could hear the missionary kids bounding up the spiral stairs. Outside in the street, the voices of women on their way to market floated by.

Then my sense of smell kicked in, and the air was thick and rich with the unique aroma of Africa. It was humid, too—so full of moisture that I knew a storm would be blowing in by early evening.

The sunlight told me it was almost dinner time. What was I making? I had forgotten, but I needed to get it started soon because Csaba would be coming up to eat. There was still all that food to unpack, and I needed to stop standing here doing nothing.

But wait, what was happening? My shoulders were shaking, and my eyes were wet. This was odd. I was standing in the middle of the room—crying. Why? It was just an ordinary day, like a thousand days before it and another thousand days that would come after it. Yet I was crying, and the tears were pooling up in the mask of the CPAP machine that I was oddly wearing while standing there in the middle of the Abidjan apartment. When had I gotten a CPAP machine? An ache was growing in my chest, and I recognized the all-too-familiar feeling of my heart grieving, mourning the lost world that I so desperately wanted to get back to.

Standing there on a normal afternoon in Africa, I cried as if my heart would break until I actively pulled myself away from apartment 15. The sounds faded away, then the people, then the details of the room, then the walls. The air around me was no longer damp but dry, and there were none of the strong odors of Africa but only mild fresh smells coming through the window. I had come back through the waters of a pool that had once been Africa and found myself in this other world called Idaho. The room around me was strangely quiet; the breathing of my husband in bed next to me was the only sound.

I sat up, pulled off my mask, and dried my eyes. Yes, my husband was there in bed; that hadn't changed. My three children still living at home were all downstairs in their rooms. That was reassuring. I wanted to be fully back in the present because the vision had been *too* real. I needed to pull myself away from the ache, the memory, the pain. I looked around the room and thanked God for the *here* and *now*. I saw my husband asleep and thanked God for him. He was always so wonderful. I kept thanking God for the things He had given to us as gifts in our lives here in Idaho, until the pain started to abate and the heaviness of leaving Africa ceased to grip my heart. I had said goodbye.

I gave the ache of all those memories up to God, as well as the disappointments, the losses, and the pain. I let God's love wash over me, healing me. I did not have any more of those visions of Africa. The past was God's now, and no longer mine to keep and cling to as though I could bring it back. The past could no longer bother me, because it was safely tucked away in God's loving arms, where all things should be. The past was a wonderful and great gift, but God had given me many gifts, and one of them was the present. I need to live here because that is where God has placed me now.

I still needed to deal with my memories of the hard times of the war, my long illness, and the pain of isolation. For those, I had to go back with the Lord by my side and give each painful memory over to Him to swallow up in His love and mercy. Only by looking at the cross and Christ's ultimate victory over sin and sorrow could I understand how my suffering connected to the whole of God's plan and how a negative memory could lose its power to hurt, engulfed and dismantled by God's glorious victory train. "For whatever is born of God overcomes the world. And this is the victory that has overcome the world—our faith. Who is he who overcomes the world, but he who believes that Jesus is the Son of God?" (1 John 5:4).

Back in the present, I took joy in my kids. Hans, that string-bean boy in my vision, had grown up into a fine young man and was married with a child on the way. Noai, now a beautiful young lady, was interested in mission work and had an active love of nature. Andreas was still a bruiser and loved to snowboard and climb mountains—the taller the better. Jeremiah, too, loved climbing things, now even in the sky. He went skydiving with some classmates and jumped out of an airplane at 13,000 feet. What was even more amazing to me was that he actually enjoyed it!

Chapter 25

Grandma's House

> He has made everything beautiful in its time. Also
> He has put eternity in their hearts. (Eccles. 3:11)

THERE WAS STILL ONE MORE GOODBYE to carry out. The last time I had been to my parents' house in Illinois was in 2006 on our return from Africa. Soon after that, my parents had sold the house and moved. With so many worlds disappearing from my life, I felt the need to see my childhood home one last time. Csaba and I went back in 2014 for my father's funeral, and Noai came with us.

We rounded the corner to Second Avenue and saw the familiar red brick house. At the sight of it, a flood of memories came back. It felt like any other time coming back from Africa, but this time the place wasn't ours anymore. The yard was the same, except that there was a strange woman raking leaves on *our* lawn. Mom greeted her and asked if we could poke around. She told us to help ourselves, so we ambled around to the backyard. The huge maple that the kids used to climb to sit and play their whistles was half dead, damaged by a storm, but the flower beds the squirrels played in were just the same, and the cherry tree had grown.

"Noai, isn't this weird?" I asked her. "Doesn't it make you want to open the back door and go inside?"

Noai said, "Yes, and eat cantaloupe and sit by the window on the round squeaky chairs that swivel."

It felt like nothing had changed and we should be going inside soon—but there was a boat in the driveway, and it was no longer *our* house. I was so thankful that God had allowed me to grow up there. The good memories of this home would live on—raking leaves, climbing the maple tree, eating on the back porch, enjoying the flowers. Yet all the change and life moving faster than I wanted it to made me long for eternity, where there would be no more goodbyes or moving on, but a true home that would remain forever. God gives our hearts a longing for something more than we can find on this earth, since it is not our true home. Occasionally, there are moments that cause a greater longing for that *something more*. This was one of those moments for us.

Hans later wrote to me of his own experience with this kind of longing. "I looked to the sky and saw the sunset on the horizon in its gentlemanly evening dress, preparing to retire. The sun was a ball of soft fire, the scattered clouds were starting to blush, and I walked up the hill just as the fire lit all the wispy fingerlets that warmed their hands over the sun's dying heat. It's in times like these, beholding some splendor in nature, that . . . a window is opened up in the heart for a brief moment longing for heaven and eternity, more than usual in everyday life."

Hard as this mortal life can be, God has given His love to bear us through the tough times, laughter to sweeten them, and His strength to carry us in even our darkest moments. We don't know what life will bring on any day, but we know who we are journeying with.

Chapter 26

Memories and Microwaves

IN 2013, CSABA MADE ANOTHER TRIP TO Ivory Coast to work with the team while the rest of us remained in Idaho. In our village house, he had the odd feeling that time had stopped when we left eleven years earlier. The whole house, never packed up after our departure, lay frozen in time. Hans' clay pillars were still on his desk waiting to be finished. They had been meant for his miniature buildings down by the pond, but the buildings had been washed away by the rains years ago. Andreas' old, tangled fishing line was still in the closet waiting to be used in a pond that was now filling up with silt. Jeremiah's

Matchbox cars lay in a heap on the shelf. Noai's wicker doll furniture was piled in the corner, waiting for her to come back. Mice had gotten into her shelf and made nests in her stuffed animals.

Csaba didn't want to touch the children's things. It seemed better to leave them until they could come back and go through it themselves. Besides, an entire people group here still needed the Bible—there was much work for him to do.

"I woke at 4 a.m. and couldn't get back to sleep," he wrote to me. "I felt burdened for the Bakwés' salvation with the rise of Islam all around. Firmain says that Muslim evangelists came to our village to invite people to the mosque. We have to pray for the fledgling Bakwé church that the Scriptures will feed, mature, and equip the Bakwé for the rough years ahead. Christ's love is the answer. First, the Bakwé need to experience that love; then they need to practice it among themselves, their churches, and their neighbors. That love will conquer. Joyful, thankful, loving Christians present such a contrast to those without the Spirit. We also need to pray for faithful teaching of the Word as we get it translated."

On this trip, Csaba had the translation of Acts checked by a consultant; then he and Alexis drafted 1 Corinthians. After a month of hard work, Csaba returned home. It was good to have him back. He continued on with his Bakwé work at the office in Moscow, contacting his team via the internet and solving the various problems that came up.

While he was occupied with this, I was dealing with my own problems—those of microwaves and parrots.

Our African Grey parrot had perfected his imitation of the microwave's high-pitched beep. He repeated it so well and so often that it drove me crazy. I needed to get it out of his vocabulary! The only way to do this was to buy a new microwave. When our old one finally broke, I went to Walmart on a quest for a parrot-proof microwave. I perused the microwave options with some uncertainty. Which one's sound would I want repeated *ad nauseam*? I tried reading the boxes but found nothing helpful, so I located an employee to assist me. I told him my sole criteria for the new microwave: something with a sound that wouldn't drive me crazy when my parrot repeated it. The employee looked at me quizzically, then burst out laughing. I defended my position by saying that the parrot imitated the ring tone of our phone, too, and I'd had to change that three times as well. When I told him about the problem we'd had with the parrot after the smoke alarm went off, he laughed so hard that I wasn't sure if I was going to be helped or not.

Once he regained his composure, the testing began. The only way to try out the microwaves was to lug each one three aisles over to a socket. The first microwave had a *very* loud, high-pitched sound. I shook my head. "No way." We went back and got a black one off the shelf. It, too, had the same high-pitched sound, and besides that my parrot hates the color black. Off he went to get the next machine.

By this time, another woman had come to look at the microwaves. "Oh good," she exclaimed, "What have you found out about the microwaves?"

I told her that my criteria were likely to be different from hers. When asked what they were, I told her about my parrot. She looked at me incredulously and burst out laughing. "That is hysterical! You're picking a microwave based on your parrot? I've never heard of anything so funny in my life."

I told her about the phone's ring tone and the smoke alarm. We left her in hysterics as we went off to test the third machine. Another employee walked by and gave us a quizzical look. I told the new guy that this operation was crucial to my sanity.

The third machine had a lower, softer sound. I said, "This is it!"

We wheeled that one back to the microwave aisle where the other woman was waiting. "Is it a go? Does it pass the parrot test?" I put both thumbs up.

At this, she nearly collapsed in laughter (again). "I still don't believe it! You have absolutely made my day." My helper was laughing, too. I told him I'd give him a good report up at customer service for going above and beyond the call of duty. I wrote down the name of the machine and took the good news back to Csaba.

Csaba came to check it out but saw how small it was and decided against it. We went to an appliance store to look for more options. Again I found an employee and told him our absurd criteria. He said he had just the machine. It was a large white microwave with the one feature that I really, *really* wanted—a mute button. Relieved, we brought our new microwave home and waited for the sound of the old microwave to stop haunting us as the parrot's recall memory faded.

Chapter 27

The Return

> The echo of laughter and bare feet on cold stone; sun-baked tar roof, past the sound of bottle-caps, past the smell of soap and drying laundry; dry, dusty storage sheds, full of secrets. (Andreas)

IN JUNE 2014, OUR CHURCH PAID FOR us to return to Ivory Coast to provide us some closure. We hadn't been to the village since 2002. Hans, now married with kids, stayed behind in Idaho, but the rest of us made that long-awaited trip at last.

The morning after we arrived in Abidjan, we woke to the brilliant sunshine and rich, thick humidity we had known so well before. Abidjan was so different now from when we had last seen it. The shops outside the administration center were open, and people were everywhere. It was as if there had been no war.

Walking around the missionary guesthouse was like going down memory lane, each area bringing back its own special memories. The kids went out into the yard to visit their old haunts. The ancient spreading tree behind the building had been cut down, the sandbox where they had constructed ancient Egyptian cities was now a dumping place for old furniture, and the carving of the antelope nursing its young by the entrance was gone, but it was still *wonderful* to see the place again.

June is the month of the heaviest rains, and, unfortunately, when we left for the village in the morning, it was pouring. Travel was difficult as we dodged potholes on the four-lane highway. Adding to the trouble were the cars on the other side jumping the median and driving on our side of the street (straight at us!) due to the backed-up traffic on their side. We turned off that chaotic road to take another route—but this road proved worse, because the rain was so heavy that we couldn't tell how deep the potholes were until we drove into them.

We commented to each other as we went, "Wow, look at how far down that tanker went in that pothole! Do you think we'll make it?"

"Our truck is sinking!"

"Watch out! Another tree down on the road!"

Thankfully, we made it safely to San-Pédro, where we were to stay at the Assemblies of God guesthouse. This had been looted in 2004 by the same armed gang we had been trying to avoid during our stay at the CMA guesthouse nearby. The Assemblies of God missionary who had been there at the time had evacuated with the rest of the French, but she later returned, and the guesthouse had been refitted and was running again.

After enjoying the beach in all its glory for a few days (with me able to swim!), we went on to the village, where we were joyfully welcomed back by our workers, Janvier, Bibionay, and Moise the gardener, plus a whole herd of Bakwé kids. The next morning, we did the customary greeting tour around the village. In each courtyard, people gave the Bakwé cry of delight and shook our hands, exclaiming loudly, "Your wife is back! She was sick and look, now she is here! We thank God."

Yes, we were back! As we traveled from courtyard to courtyard, we picked up quite the entourage of children, which grew larger and rowdier as we proceeded, circling us in a jostling, playful group. Then we headed home, the entourage completely enveloping us. I was reminded how much living in an Ivorian village is like drinking from a fire hose. You don't get just a sip, but the full blast of colorful, noisy humanity.

Next, Csaba met with the translation team to discuss their plans for the week while our kids explored the property, climbed trees, chopped through the tangled bush with machetes, or just sat quietly by the pond.

As I walked around the yard, my mind played tricks on me. I came upon the mongoose cage and almost thought I saw two furry animals inside. But the mongooses had died years ago, and the cage was empty and falling apart. I went up the path expecting to see our little backyard guesthouse and did a double take when I found only ruins. It had fallen due to heavy rains. Time had frozen the village in our minds, and we were being jolted to the present by this trip.

As we sat and talked with the villagers on our front porch, we found out that some of those who were most resistant to Christianity had died, and their children or grandchildren were now attending church. We also discovered that many people had cell phones now, which meant there was a real potential of getting the Scriptures recorded and into the hands of the common people through a phone app.

It was fun to chat with visitors for whom time seemed to have no meaning. It was good to sit and hear their stories and see their faces light up with Bakwé expressions of delight. But since there was a lot to do, Csaba often had to slip away to the office. During this visit, he worked with his team to finish the corrections on the translations of 1 and 2 Thessalonians, Ephesians, Colossians, and Philippians. Then they began drafting 1 Peter. After Peter's epistles, he would have only four books left to translate in the New Testament.

THE RETURN

It felt so good to be back. We did all the things we used to do: fishing, camping, hiking on the mountain, swimming in the ocean, and visiting friends. It was good for the kids to see their old toys and rooms and pack them up. At the end of our stay, we left Ivory Coast with the peace of having finally laid that chapter of our lives to rest. The unsettled feeling of being ripped away from our old life was now resolved. I thanked God for giving the children the chance to close this chapter of their lives.[1]

Yes, it was good to go back and see the village once more, but it was also good to return to our permanent home in Idaho. Looking back, God had given us, truly, the best of both worlds.

---

1. Why did we not move back to the village? For a number of reasons. First, when an African country goes through a war, the aftereffects of unrest are hard to predict, so you usually wait a while to bring back the families. It took a long time for the country to be stable enough to return permanently. By that time, a large number of our support staff had moved to Mali to run things from that center, meaning we no longer had sufficient support in Ivory Coast. Second, my health was still fragile. I have recovered, but I still live in the low range of normal. Living in an Ivorian village takes a lot of strength, and I don't have much stamina. Third, by the time the coutry had settled down, our kids were older and needed better schooling. We did not want to separate the family by sending them to boarding school (a common solution for missionary families). And, finally, Csaba had already been running the project from afar, and it was working. We have adjusted to our new life in the States, and time has healed a lot of the grief of leaving.

Chapter 28
Noai

> It is better to be sick providing Christ come to the bedside and draw the curtains, and say, Courage, I am thy salvation, than to enjoy health being lusty and strong and never to be visited by God. (Samuel Rutherford)

LIVING IN THE STATES AWAY FROM tropical diseases, threat of war, and harsh living conditions was not without its own severe trials. Partway through college at New Saint Andrews, Noai developed double vision. We had her eyes checked but found nothing wrong. The doctor ordered an MRI and again found nothing conclusive—just one small brain lesion he thought was probably from a virus. Noai's eyes went back to normal within a week, and we were thankful that the affliction seemed to have passed. But a vague funny feeling remained in her eyes throughout the year, and we returned to the ophthalmologist. The doctor concluded that the problem wasn't her eyes but the nerves behind them and suggested that we see a neurologist. This meant expensive tests, so we decided to wait until we had clear evidence of a need for it. Some months later, her left leg felt weird. We prayed, and that went away, too, but she began to have other odd symptoms: random muscle weakness, distorted vision, and toes going numb. These things came and went, but we wondered if they were all connected.

We prayed that God would make it clear what we should do. Within a week, half of Noai's face went numb. That was our answer, and we made an appointment to see a neurologist. Noai had an extensive MRI and a spinal tap. She was diagnosed with multiple sclerosis (MS), a progressive autoimmune disease caused by the body attacking the myelin sheaths around the nerves, damaging their relay capacity. She was referred to a specialist for treatment.

This was crushing news. I struggled to cope with the fact that my beautiful daughter might be headed for severe incapacitation or an early death. We'd had a hard life and were no strangers to trials. When God had struck me with years of devastating fatigue, He had given me Noai to help. But now *she* was the one being hit. Would the very person who has served me so much and given so faithfully now be the one needing help herself? "Why Lord?" I asked. "Is this the reward for all her sacrifice? Aren't You being a bit harsh?"

It certainly seemed so at the time. In one swoop, God had taken away the potential for so many things: long life, health, perhaps even children. Her future was no longer bright. She might never marry, or have a family, or be able to go to the mission field (one of her strongest desires). I grieved for her and for what she could lose. I prayed to God for mercy, pleading that He would give her back her life just as He did for Hezekiah when he prayed (Isa. 38). I had to remind myself that God loved her more than we did, and that even if He took precious things away from her, He would give her more of Himself in return. Csaba and I had always prayed that our children would glorify God in their lives, and it looked like God was taking a very special route to answer that prayer. We just needed to trust Him.

After all our questions were asked and given over to God, we were determined to accept what He had given Noai and choose to follow Him unreservedly, giving our amen to His will. We prayed and asked for mercy and help in doing this, because we were going to need it. Then we cried because it was hard, but when we cried, we cried in hope with those everlasting arms underneath.[1]

---

1. "The eternal God is your refuge, and underneath are the everlasting arms" (Deut. 33:27).

> This I recall to my mind, therefore I have hope. Through the LORD's mercies we are not consumed, because His compassions fail not. They are new every morning; great is your faithfulness. "The LORD is my portion," says my soul, "Therefore I hope in Him!" The LORD is good to those who wait for him, to the soul who seeks Him.... For the Lord will not cast off forever. Though He causes grief, yet He will show compassion according to the multitude of His mercies. For He does not afflict willingly, nor grieve the children of men. (Lam. 3:21–24, 31–33)

Noai still had to deal with the death of all her dreams. God was asking her to trust Him, to place each of her desires on His altar as a sacrifice and follow Him.

Seeing the struggle she was having with this, I asked her, "What do you really want from life? Do you want only *your* ideal? What if you had a real choice between your ideal life and God's wild path? Which would you choose? Say the ideal path ends in a milquetoast life, while God's wild path came with all the glory of His goodness and blessing through the hardships? And say these blessings would be wilder, realer, and more precious than anything you could have gotten any other way? Which would you choose?"

Noai said she would choose God's wild path over her ideal one.

"Good. When you get to heaven, you will understand all God did and will be able to give your amen to it then. So you might as well give your amen to it *now* and be credited with faith, because once you can see, it is no longer faith, and that opportunity will be lost."

She did, and was filled with God's peace and joy.

We went to her first appointment with the MS specialist, where we learned there were new drugs on the market that could change the course of the disease. If a particular drug was effective in her treatment, it could slow her physical decline and extend a good quality of life. Since MS is an unpredictable disease, we couldn't know for sure how things would go, but these advances in medicine provided some hope of an almost-normal life.

We tried the first drug recommended by the specialist but discovered after a few months that it wasn't working, because Noai continued to experience neurological attacks. We were in Wallowa County, Oregon, hiking in the mountains and enjoying the majestic splendor of God's creation, when Noai mentioned that she was having more eye trouble. I suddenly felt a deep sorrow creeping over what had been a perfectly glorious day.

I realized that we couldn't take these pleasures for granted anymore. Each day is a gift given us for that day alone, and we needed to keep thanking God for what we have right now. God would take care of all Noai's tomorrows. All we needed to do was rest in His faithfulness today.

We tried another drug, but that didn't work, either, and the prognosis for her future wasn't good. Each time we went back for an appointment, we heard more bad news. For days afterward, we would feel a heaviness until we could successfully hand it back to the Lord to carry. It was a process, but as we grew in our faith and trust in God, that process became shorter. We even made a game of seeing how quickly we could give bad news back to Him to the point where we could sing, not carrying the weight of this trouble in our hearts a moment longer.

A few years into this, the Women of Hope prayer group wanted to do something special for Noai. For the next appointment, they gave us a couple of gifts that she was to open during the day. We always tried to make appointment days special to offset the overwhelming negatives they tended to bring, and these gifts would make it extra special. On the day of the appointment, we read a humorous P. G. Wodehouse story. Noai opened her first present in the car and was delighted with it. Just being remembered meant so much.

While she was in the MRI, Csaba and I dashed off to do some shopping and brought back a gift of two owl candles. Noai has a great love for all things *bird*, so we were sure she would enjoy them. I wanted to give her the second present from the group right after she got the results of the MRI, but we forgot all about it when the doctor told us that the most recent drug hadn't worked, either, and Noai would be confined to a wheelchair in five years if we didn't find an effective drug very soon. The doctor suggested we step up to the biggest gun they had in medicine, but it was dangerous and could prove fatal under certain conditions. She was to get a test to see if she had those conditions.

As we left the doctor's office, we felt numb. There was so much to think about. That heavy weight was back over our heads and hearts again. We went to a clinic to get her tested, and as we drove away from the clinic, we started to sing:

> Great is Thy Faithfulness, O God my Father,
> There is no shadow of turning with Thee;
> Thou changest not, Thy compassions they fail not;
> As Thou hast been, Thou forever wilt be.
>
> Great is Thy faithfulness, Great is Thy faithfulness,
> Morning by morning new mercies I see.
> All I have needed Thy hand hath provided,
> Great is Thy faithfulness, Lord, unto me.

We sang falteringly at first, but with greater ease as the truth of the hymn lifted our spirits. There was something reassuring about those words reminding us that God's own dear presence would cheer and guide, providing everything we could possibly need. The weight lifted within minutes, even though this had been the worst news yet. Noai opened her last present and was delighted.

In the end, the positives of the day swallowed up that enormous negative. Noai thanked us for making the day so special. She was ready to look to God to help her face her condition and move forward one day at a time. This wasn't the end of her hard times. There would be many more days in the future when she needed to refocus and look up to God once more. But He was there for her every day, and on the days when the unknown and scary future became the present, He took her hand and walked her through every step for His glory.

She did take that scary drug, and it halted the progression of her MS for a time. God had given her back her life, for the present. The future was in His hands.

Chapter 29
Kellen

A daughter at birth is like a diamond in the rough. When you are given this precious gem, you take great care to form it, making sure each cut in the process is just right. Bit by bit, the rough stone is transformed into a beautiful and brightly shining gem in your hand. As you enjoy the brilliance of your diamond, you feel that all the sweat and tears, all the time and care, were worth it.

You guard that diamond carefully since it is precious to you. But as the diamond shines in your hand, others notice it, too. One day, a young man is captivated by its beauty and feels he can't live without it.

Then he does a bold thing. He asks you for your diamond, even though he did nothing to bring it to its present magnificence. But what is stranger still, if you deem him a prince among men, you give him your diamond. He takes this precious gift and sets it in his crown to shine brightly. The cherished light reflected from within its depths helps him to truly be the prince he was meant to be.[1]

IN MAY 2014, I WAS GETTING THE MAIL and saw a letter addressed to Csaba from Kellen Meyer, the son of our friends Matt and Renae. Kellen had recently graduated from college and was working in California. Because I knew he was interested in missions, I opened the letter. But it wasn't about missions; it was about our daughter. He was asking to court her. My first thought was that this was fantastic. But then I wondered how Noai would react. She had shot down all attempts from other young men who had asked the same thing. Besides, Kellen was four years younger than Noai. Our families had been close since our return to the States in 2006, and she looked on Kellen almost as a younger brother.

I showed Csaba the letter, and he told me that he had previously noticed what a fine man Kellen was and had thought he would make a good husband for someone.

---

1. I wrote this for Noai's wedding. Several mothers have told me they found it helpful to them in processing the giving away of their own "diamonds."

Csaba told Noai that someone had asked to court her.

"Who?"

"I'm not telling you until you promise to pray about it before answering."

After she said she would do that, Csaba told her it was Kellen.

She responded, "Aw, that's so sweet of him."

I thought to myself, "This isn't getting off to a great start."

Csaba told Noai that he truly respected Kellen. Noai said she also respected Kellen—too much to give him an automatic *no*. She would pray about it first, then say *no*.

Csaba talked to Kellen over the phone and asked him if he knew what he would be getting himself into with Noai having MS. Kellen researched the disease, prayed about it, and wrestled with the situation. He reported back that he was confident that if God was indeed leading him to Noai, then God would enable him to deal with everything that came their way. The prospect of a wife in a wheelchair was not a dealbreaker. Kellen told Csaba it would be a privilege to take it all on.

Unbeknownst to her, Kellen had been interested in Noai years before. His interest in her (and girls in general) had gotten distracting enough that he made a vow not to think about a woman until a year after he graduated from college. He finished his degree and took a job in California. During this time, he prayed for Noai, for her MS, and that she would find a good husband.

When the vow was up, Kellen set about making a list of the qualities he was looking for in a wife. Noai's name kept coming up in his mind as he was working on it, so he wrote her name down on the side for consideration. After talking with his father and praying about it, Kellen wrote the letter to Csaba.

A year earlier, Jim Wilson, our pastor's father, had sat Kellen's father Matt down and said, "Kellen is going to marry Noai." He later told Noai (who worked for both Jim and Matt at Community Christian Ministries) to expect to have a guy within a year. When she asked him if he had someone in mind, he must have forgotten his previous pronouncement, because he said *no*. In fact, no one even knew about Jim's bold statement until Matt recounted the story the night before the wedding. God hadn't forgotten Noai. He was preparing just the right man for her.

Some time had passed since she had last seen Kellen, and as she was considering his letter that afternoon, all that Noai remembered of him was that he had a good character, was fun-loving, and liked doing the same things she did. But he was on the shorter side, with a big, boyish grin and a hearty laugh. Noai's template for husband material was different: someone tall and very serious, and she was supposed to fall for him in romantic, chick-flick style. This business with Kellen was not according to her plans.

In an effort to shake the uncomfortable feeling of turmoil that was quickly welling up inside her, Noai immediately sought ways of knocking Kellen out of the running. First, she turned to her older brother, expecting Hans to find the notion absurd—and was surprised to learn that he was all for it. When her close friend Lisa Just came by to visit that evening, she found Noai in a pool of tears in the kitchen. Astonished, Lisa asked what was wrong, and Noai responded that Kellen had asked her out. Lisa had to stifle a laugh at hearing such *dire* news! Noai asked her what she thought of the match, but Lisa said that she didn't know Kellen well enough to have an opinion.

Since the decision wasn't being made clear by these responses, Noai sought other excuses to settle her mind. She told Lisa that she really needed someone who could play guitar to accompany her on the Irish whistle. And as far as she knew, Kellen didn't play the guitar. Case closed! Now she could go back to her tranquil life. But the inner turmoil didn't go away like she had hoped. She didn't like everyone else's positive responses to the idea of her and Kellen, but, for some odd reason, *she* couldn't say no to him, either.

Finally, she agreed to email back and forth with Kellen. To her surprise, she found she enjoyed it quite a bit. Later, Kellen asked to talk with her on the phone. She agreed but planned to end the relationship at the conclusion of the first call so as not to lead him on. They talked on for an hour. She enjoyed the conversation so much that she decided to keep him in the running—for now.

Csaba and I decided to have Kellen surprise her with a visit to see how she would react to him in person. We took her for a hike up Moscow Mountain, a few miles away from our house. We walked up to one of the ponds and hung out for a bit. Suddenly, Noai was startled by a loud, high-pitched shrieking coming from the bushes. She thought it might be a cougar! Instead, it was Kellen, who had made a whistle out of a blade of grass held tightly between his thumbs. He popped out and walked toward her with a confident gait and his characteristic grin. She was surprised to see him but pleased at the same time. She noticed that he was much *taller* than she'd remembered, more solid, more manly, but still had that same boyish smile. We left them to hike and talk. Later, Noai said they'd had a wonderful time and that being with him felt like the most natural thing in the world.

That evening, Lisa came over for a visit. When she walked in, Kellen was out on the back patio playing—you guessed it—a guitar. There went another excuse. It didn't take Lisa long to see where this was going. After only a few minutes of being around Kellen, she was sure he was the one for Noai. "I know how this story ends," she thought, followed by, "Oh dear—how am I going to tell Noai?" Lisa had been the only one who hadn't given an immediate *hurray* to the idea of their relationship. Now she was fully on board, too.

In the meantime, Noai was having an odd battle with herself. She felt the whole thing should end because Kellen still wasn't the future husband she'd pictured. At the same time, she was really enjoying getting reacquainted with him. To settle this inner confusion, Noai made a list of the reasons why Kellen *wouldn't do*. It was hard going, since she couldn't find any serious arguments against him, and the list turned a little humorous. He liked kidney beans, but she preferred garbanzos. (Terrible!) He wasn't poetic, she claimed. (A few days later, a bouquet showed up at the door with an original poem attached.) She thought he couldn't spell very well. (I reminded her that *she* couldn't spell, either. She shot back, "Well, one of us has to!" I asked if she'd heard of something called spellcheck.)

I knew she was scraping the bottom of the barrel because she was scared of finding him a real prospect, which was not according to plan. Kellen was a friend, and he was not supposed to be anything else! She wanted God to make that clear to everyone, herself included, and He apparently wasn't cooperating.

Seeing her struggle, Csaba and I asked her if she wanted to end the relationship. She quietly said, "Not yet."

At one point, when she was again feeling doubts, Justine, Hans' wife and Noai's good friend, reminded her that God was not the God of confusion. God would not leave her unprotected or in a situation that was not right when she looked to Him. He would lead her to the very best, and if He continued to lead her to Kellen, it would be good. God could be trusted.

Noai realized she wasn't trusting God. She was fighting Him and listening only to her emotions, which kept fluctuating.

Throughout this time, Csaba and I saw that Noai acted very much in love. But she would not admit to it since she still didn't have the high romantic emotions that she thought indicated true love.

I told her that love is like an iceberg. Above the water are the romantic feelings, and underneath are the solid, lasting things that make for a great marriage: respect, deep caring, and friendship. She was judging by what she felt on the surface, while underneath the churning water of her emotions the iceberg was growing deeper and deeper with what really counted. She was just looking at the wrong side.

Noai turned to our pastor Doug and his wife Nancy for counsel. They gave Noai advice similar to Justine's: God never leads His children through doubts. There are *questions* that can and should be answered to determine if someone is right or not, but *doubts* are vague and unanswerable. You can't rely on them to be your guide. You need to look to God in faith for real answers, expecting that He will give them.

Over the course of the summer, Kellen's unshakeable confidence in the face of Noai's vacillating emotions, his surety in looking to God, and his cheerful steadiness through various hardships were slowly drawing her in. He didn't seem to be phased by anything.

In the fall, Noai went to visit Jim Wilson, who was well-known for his wise counsel. His son Doug, our pastor, was there doing his father's finances. In the middle of telling Jim about her fluctuating emotions over this whole affair, Doug interrupted. "Noai, does it feel like you're playing chess with God?"

She said, "Yeah!"

Doug chuckled. "You know, you can't win!"

Shortly after this, Csaba told Noai that she couldn't keep stringing Kellen along. He needed to know if this was heading toward marriage or not. If not, Kellen should be free to find someone else.

Noai had known this was coming, and the thought of making the decision scared her. I asked her to think about it this way: "Remember the time Kellen asked you to jump off the cliff into the river, and you did it together? Well, you'll be jumping off the cliff holding God's hand and being caught on the other end by Kellen's."

Csaba told her that he would give her one week to pray about it, and at the end of the week he only wanted to know one thing: if she thought God was in it.

During her week of praying, Kellen called her every night as usual. They talked of adventures. She realized she didn't want to miss out on any future adventures with him. They talked of suffering and death, and she felt a grip on her heart that she wanted to be with him when he died. It dawned on her that she was already deeply in love with him, and it hadn't come from romantic emotions but from a deep, caring respect and a desire to be by his side throughout life.

All her doubts left, and when Kellen said his usual "I love you" at the end of their conversation, for the first time she said, "I love you, too," then quickly hung up.

Kellen called her back right away. "I heard that!"

So now there was peace. Noai knew that even if her nerves made her emotional again, Kellen would be there to catch her. She didn't know when he would propose, but she knew what her answer would be.

Kellen wanted to make the proposal a surprise, so while Noai was visiting him in California, he took her out to eat, then suggested they go to a nearby dam to get a photo.

When they arrived at the park, the ranger said the gate would be closing in fifteen minutes. They ran out to the middle of the dam, and Kellen set up his camera.

The ranger yelled, "You've got ten minutes!"

Kellen was thinking, "Be patient, man! I'm trying to get engaged!"

He dashed over to Noai, got down on one knee, and asked her to marry him. She said *yes*, and he picked her up and swung her around and around, with the ranger yelling in the background, "Five minutes!"

They grabbed the camera and sprinted back to the car. But Kellen was so happy he couldn't find his way out of the parking lot, and they spun the car around and around laughing until they finally found the exit. They were engaged!

God gave Noai the hard providence of multiple sclerosis, but He also gave her a gift to help her through it—a precious gift that she kept trying to give back. In the end, she found it to be the most wonderful gift He had ever given her apart from His Son Jesus Christ. She has looked back on this happy providence as an Ebenezer stone (1 Samuel 7:12) signifying God's unfailing love and care for His children. Noai and Kellen were married the following spring. In the years since, Kellen has been by her side, encouraging her and pointing her to the joy and riches we have in Christ. God has been there to help them every step of the way, just as He promised. "And the LORD, He is the One who goes before you. He will be with you, He will not leave you nor forsake you; do not fear nor be dismayed" (Deut. 31:8).

Chapter 30

Finished

> He who continually goes forth weeping, bearing seed for sowing, shall doubtless come again with rejoicing, bringing his sheaves with him. (Ps. 126:6)

DURING OUR YEARS IN IDAHO, CSABA has returned to Ivory Coast once or twice a year to check on the translation team. Though progress was slow and the work proved difficult from such a distance, the translation continued to move ahead. In April 2017, Csaba made another trip to have 2 Peter, Jude, and Revelation checked by the translation consultants. In July, he took me back with him for a month to see the completion of the last book to be translated, the Gospel of Matthew.

Returning to the village felt different for me this time. The last visit had been both a joyful reunion and a nostalgic memorial as the kids and I said goodbye to our past life. But this was a new era, and we were getting the house upgraded with new furniture covers and curtains and repairing things that were broken. It was now ready for the dedication celebration and would be more comfortable for Csaba's visits.

The team worked hard on the checking and made good progress. They went over each verse word by word and looked at whether they had used the most suitable words or phrases. It was a painstaking process, and sometimes there were heated discussions, but in the end they found the best words available.

Life in Africa is hard and unpredictable. There were many setbacks in the translation work over the years (our evacuation being the biggest but by no means the only one), and this visit was no exception. Firmain's son was in a motorcycle accident and had to be taken to the hospital, which took Firmain out of the office for a day. Then our gardener, Moise, passed away unexpectedly due to severe and chronic health problems. During the last week of intense work, one of Perez's relatives died. We expected Perez to be gone for the funeral from that point on, but his relatives decided to put it off for a week. God was watching out for us.

On the final day of checking, Csaba called me to come to the office to witness the completion of the New Testament. Alexis read the last verses of Matthew in Bakwé: "Jesu nya

FINISHED

jijrö 'üün gba 'ɔ nëma: 'Nyɔsʋa nyɩ 'mɩ tʋtʋ nyra cɛlɩa 'kama 'klüa 'fıɔ. 'Ii känyrı, 'ba mi tʋtʋ gälıa glügbüa 'fıɔa nyɛɛ, 'ba nrörö 'üün 'na 'wʋnyɛrɛnyüü 'lɩ, 'ba 'pa 'üün 'nɩ 'wli Tʋa 'nyrɩklɩ, 'Jʋa 'nyrɩklɩ nyra 'Nyüna Susua 'nyrɩklɩ, 'kä 'a 'kpɩa 'üün wiili kä 'fıɔ 'n gbala kä 'amɩ, 'ia 'lɩträäräkʋ. 'Mɔɔlɔ nɩ, 'ba jresaa 'n bä 'ana tɔrʋpɩɔ sɔ 'saarɩ gälɩ a 'tɔ 'pläa bɩarafa 'wʋ. 'Asɩ i bä!'" ("Then Jesus came and spoke to them, saying, 'All authority has been given to Me in heaven and on earth. Go therefore and make disciples of all nations, baptizing them in the name of the Father and of the Son and of the Holy Spirit, teaching them to observe all things that I have commanded you; and lo, I am with you always, even to the end of the age. Amen'" Matt. 28:18–20.)

Then Pastor Firmain translated it back into French so that Yegbé Antoine, the translation consultant, could make sure everything was correct. When Yegbé was satisfied, he looked up and exclaimed, "Glory be to God. We're done with the New Testament!"

Everyone broke out singing, first with a French hymn and then with a Bakwé one. Then we held hands as Pastor Désiré[1] prayed, "Thank You, Lord, for You have not forgotten the Bakwé, but have blessed them with Your Word. Thank You for the team and all those who have worked together to make it happen. Through many hardships and trials, You have sustained us, and we were able to finish. May it be powerfully used for Your glory."

---

1. A Bakwé pastor who is part of Csaba's translation team.

I was thankful for the opportunity to be there with Csaba at the completion of this first stage of our life's work. Being able to finish the New Testament was a great blessing because so much had gone wrong throughout. By God's grace, He saw us through!

Chapter 31

The Final Readthrough

> That is what mortals misunderstand. They say of some temporal suffering, "No future bliss can make up for it," not knowing that Heaven, once attained, will work backwards and turn even that agony into a glory. (C.S. Lewis, *The Great Divorce*)

CSABA'S NEXT TASK WAS PREPARING THE manuscript for publication. This complicated process included writing a general introduction, individual book introductions, and a glossary of terms; translating names on the maps that were to be included; correcting spelling and punctuation; and adding references, footnotes, and more.

We returned to Ivory Coast in January 2018 to read through the entire New Testament out loud with the Bakwé review committee, composed of people from each of the local churches. After that, the manuscript would be typeset in Abidjan. Then it would go off for printing!

After a few days in Abidjan, our coworkers at the administration center prayed for us, and we headed out. The first part of the trip to the village went smoothly even though the traffic was aggressive. The second part had less traffic, but more potholes. We dodged holes, shallow and deep, for two hours. Sometimes we veered into the oncoming lane to avoid a pothole on our side as cars from the opposite direction did the same to us.

As we lurched down repeatedly into pothole after pothole, we heard the sound of metal crunching on metal. Finally, one of the tires blew. We pulled off to the side of the road. Csaba got out to examine the tire and declared it ruined. He got the spare and cranked the jack, only to have it stop midway up. Alexis also tried the jack but declared it dead. Great. There were no towns or gas stations in sight. We were in the middle of nowhere with vehicles whizzing by us at dangerously high speeds. We needed to solve our tire problem soon; once it was dark, the bandits would come out.

We flagged down a bus, but the driver said his jack was broken as well. Finally, a car pulled over and asked what was wrong. The driver, who turned out to be a mechanic, put his jack under our truck and tried to get the spare on, but it wouldn't go.

As he worked on it, I prayed. I did not want to spend the night out there with malaria mosquitos, bandits, and all. Finally, the spare went on. Everyone was relieved—until we saw that the spare was low on air.

Our good Samaritan told us that the nearest town wasn't too far off, so we drove very slowly on an almost flat tire to his shop. He gave the spare some air, and we were able to continue on our way, thanking God for getting us out of our predicament.

We rolled into the village in the evening. I was exhausted and wanted to go straight to bed, but we smelled a dead rat in the bedroom ceiling, which rendered the air in the room toxic. We set up our bed in another room, but sleep eluded me because loud music with a frantic beat was playing somewhere close enough to be unbearable. I slipped in earplugs, put a pillow over my head, and finally fell into a fitful sleep.

We spent Sunday resting up, and on Monday we got ready for the readthrough. Csaba and the Bakwé team went to town to buy food for the event. Soon, people started arriving. One woman sat on our porch while we waited for the men to return. All was peaceful until a green mamba, one of the world's most venomous snakes, fell out of a nearby tree and slithered quickly in her direction. Hearing her shrieking, I came outside and invited her into the house to sit as the snake slipped away out of sight.

When Csaba returned, he went to the office to print out the New Testament for each reader—but the printer wouldn't print. When I went in to see if he wanted lunch, he said, "Can't come right now. Please pray. I can't get this thing to work, and we start in fifteen minutes!"

I went back to the house and told Janvier to pray. Janvier prayed for God to bind the devil to keep him from stopping our work, and then he confidently thanked God for His answer. The printer began working right after that.

The Bakwé committee began the review, with each person taking a turn reading out loud from the Gospel of Matthew. After each section was read, they stopped and discussed it for flow, making any necessary changes. After the first day, one of the readers, old Mr. Sognon, told Csaba, "Thank you for doing this translation for us. The Bakwé are the last in our region to get the Scriptures, and we are very grateful. This is something that will last to future generations."

By the end of the second week, they had made good progress and finished reading up through the Gospel of John. Gagné, another of the older readers, said, "The Gospel of John is so sweet to my ears."

It was fun watching the group interact with the text. When they read how Peter said he would never deny Christ, everyone laughed, knowing what he would do. When Jesus was being tried, they reacted with guttural exclamations of astonishment at the violence of the crowd. Bakwé expressions of approval were uttered when Jesus spoke back with great boldness.

It was hard work, and the team pressed on, even working on Saturday. Halfway through, the team was exhausted, and some began to fall ill. Firmain was out for three days with malaria, and Alexis, one of the main readers, also felt malaria coming on. Perez had to leave when his brother was taken to the hospital. At these setbacks, Dominique, chairman of the Bakwé translation board, exclaimed how important this work was and declared that it was critical to get the translation to the finish line. Reinforcements must be called.

Reinforcements came, and the reading kept going. As the group interacted with the text, they were gaining a sense of ownership. These were *their* Scriptures. This Word was for them.

Chapter 32
Church in the Village

WHEN SUNDAY ARRIVED, EVERYONE took a much-needed break. Church started with everyone praying out loud all at once, aided by three tall amplifiers, leaving God to sort through it all. Then the singing began. A woman called out the first line of a song, and the congregation responded with the refrain. Then the people erupted out of their seats like a human geyser and flooded toward the front, flowing in a circular dancing stream. Joyful praise, vibrant motion, and thunderous rhythm reverberated off the walls and around the room. This lasted until a cue was given; then the rapids abated, and people trickled back to their seats for the sermon.

After the vibrantly loud sermon was over, the congregation danced their offerings up to the front, tossing coins into the box with a flourish. Last came the announcements, and then church was officially over. We got up to greet people; hands were thrust at us from all sides, and we tried to catch them all, and some of them twice. After this, we went outside into the slight breeze that felt so good after hours in the sauna-like interior.

We went home with thirty children in tow, all decked out in their Sunday finery. They made a wall around us, blocking whatever cooling breeze we might otherwise have experienced. Soon I felt a little hand slip into my left hand, so I held it. Then another slipped into my right, so I held that, too. But it didn't stop there, and another little hand inched its way into my right hand to join the first. The rest of the kids were not to be denied, so more hands were added, but eventually there was just no more room. They grabbed onto my arm four hands up until a squabble broke out and one poor soul was knocked off. Another hand took its place, and we walked on in relative peace, albeit rather slowly. I looked back at Csaba and saw that he also had multiple kids holding onto each side.

Once at our home, they sat down everywhere along the porch, with two or more kids to each chair, some on the ground, and some left standing. Then they went into their *who has the right to sit where* routine. Some poor youngsters were jettisoned off their bases; others took their place until all were comfortably (or not) seated. This lasted for about five minutes, until one child reminded everyone of the fresh nuts on our trees. They exploded out of their seats and dashed away to gather nuts. Five minutes later, they returned with their prizes and munched contentedly while I got my phone out for a photo.

At this glorious prospect, pandemonium broke out as the children rearranged themselves, getting into squabbles and pushing each other out of the way until they were all in their proper rank and file, smiling for the camera. Once the portrait was taken, I showed them the photo, and they burst in a raucous group cheer.

After I went inside, screams erupted from the kids, and Janvier and Csaba hurried out to see if someone had gotten clobbered again or if it was just a snake. But it was neither. The kids pointed to a large scorpion hidden under a cement slab by the porch, close to where I had been standing. Janvier tried to kill it, but it scurried back under the slab. Great! Now there was a scorpion near the porch steps where the kids were, and we couldn't kill it.

We told the kids to leave, but some veered back to the nuts again and began fighting about something or other. We told them to leave a second time, which they reluctantly did in that gregarious group way of theirs. As I watched them go, I wondered how many of the adults living in the village now had been one of the rowdy kids who frequented our porch twenty years earlier. How many times had I told *them* to be quiet or to stop fighting? How many times had I shaken their little hands and looked into beaming faces wanting to greet me or play with that coveted tricycle that had only two wheels? Sometimes what can seem so trivial at the moment is really very important in the grander scheme of things. I wondered what an impact we had had on them. I guess we will never fully know this side of heaven.

On Monday, the reading continued. It was a race to finish before we had to leave. The readers were still tired but kept going. When they finally finished, someone led the group in song. Then they prayed and thanked the Lord for bringing the project to completion. Soon the Bakwé would have the Word of God in their own language.

We said our goodbyes and made the long trip back to the city. In Abidjan, Csaba worked to finish a number of other checks using special translation software. He saw the illustrations formatted with the text for the first time as Wycliffe's Laurel Miller did the typesetting and page layout. Once everything was right, a first draft was printed, and Alexis and Perez came to Abidjan for another readthrough, looking for final mistakes. Csaba entered their corrections, then Laurel corrected the layout and printed another proof. Csaba, Alexis, and Perez did one more readthrough. The team had been pushing hard all day and into the night.

Csaba finished his corrections on Sunday, Perez on Monday (after staying up all night), and Alexis, who was quite thorough, on Wednesday. At 3:00 p.m. on March 21, 2018, Csaba signed off on the translation in a document that stated: "I hereby declare that I am satisfied with the text of the Bakwé New Testament as it is now, that it is ready for final paging. I do not expect to make any more textual corrections."

The translation was out of our hands for the first time since we had started, nearly thirty years earlier. We returned to the States, and the final document went to Wycliffe's publishing headquarters in Dallas for a further check before being sent to the printer in South Korea. We praised God that it was finally done. All that remained was to get the Bibles into the hands of the Bakwé people.

When the package of advance copies came in the mail and we opened the box, the beautiful, gilt-edged copies of the Bakwé New Testament brought tears to our eyes. Praise God for bringing His Word to the Bakwé!

Back in Ivory Coast, Désiré and others were preparing for the arrival of the translation by traveling through the Bakwé villages to herald the completion of the New Testament and invite them to the dedication ceremony. When Désiré showed his copy of the Bible, people exclaimed with awe and delight. They were so proud to have the Scriptures in their language, and they longed to have their own copies.

Chapter 33

The Dedication

WE HELD THE BAKWÉ NEW TESTAMENT dedication in Ivory Coast on September 14, 2019. Kellen, Noai, and their two little girls were able to attend this historic moment with us.[1]

Before the event, a special cloth was made. On it was printed a circle with a picture of the Bakwé Bible and a torch behind it. Underneath was a verse in Bakwé (Acts 8:30–31) about an African who desired to understand the Word of God. Underneath that were the dates of the project: 1989–2019. Covering the rest of the cloth were all the names

---

1. If the work had been held up for even a few months longer, the country would have been shut down due to COVID, and the dedication could not have gone forward. But God had mercy, and it happened on schedule.

of the Bakwé villages on a background of blue and white. People made outfits from this cloth and wore them for the big day. They came from all over Bakwé territory and filled the schoolyard, where they sat in a semicircle of plastic chairs under shelters.

The ceremony began. Multiple choirs sang and danced to rattles. They sang songs of gratitude that told of how their time had come, because now their language was written down, and they could have God's Word. Then a portion of the Bakwé New Testament was read out loud.

Many dignitaries gave speeches. In one speech, a Bakwé man recounted the history of the African they called the Prophet Harris. A hundred years earlier, he had come from Liberia telling people to burn their fetishes, turn to God, and wait for the white man who would bring the Bible. When the Bakwé rejected his message, he pronounced a curse on the land and said that the Bakwé people would be overlooked. This proved to be true in many ways. But then the Prophet Harris went on to predict that the white man and black man would one day sit at the same table when the curse was lifted. At the end of his speech, the speaker proclaimed in a loud voice, "Now the curse has been broken! The black man and the white are eating from the same plate, and that plate is the very Word of God!"

There were cheers from the crowd. The mayor of Méadji exclaimed, "This New Testament is the biggest gift that anybody could give to the Bakwé! This book touches the deepest layer of who they are and draws them to Christ."

Pastors and elders from many churches were called forward to dedicate the New Testament. They formed a circle around the display of New Testaments and prayed over them. Then the books were handed out to dignitaries. Csaba had the honor of presenting one to the mayor. A choir came dancing toward us. We got up and danced out to greet them; then everyone joined in the dance, and the schoolyard was filled with joyful movement. Lastly, boxes of New Testaments were brought out, and people came forward to purchase them.

After the ceremony, a plentiful feast was served, and people dispersed to various locations to eat. One Christian Bakwé chief had donated a cow and had it butchered for the occasion. We ate in our dining room with the Abidjan delegation: Wycliffe missionaries, Ivorian staff, and translators from other language projects who made the trip out to celebrate with us.

At the conclusion of the day's festivities, a Bakwé man came up to Csaba with a look of deep emotion on his face. "There are tears in my heart," he said.

Chapter 34

As the Waters Cover the Sea

> For the earth shall be filled with the knowledge of the glory of the LORD, as the waters cover the sea. (Habakkuk 2:14)

GLORY TO GOD FOR GIVING US HIS WORD! As I hold the Bakwé Bible in my hands, memories flood in, and I think about what it means to have this book. Looking back at the sweat and tears, the hard times and good, the sickness and danger, I see God triumphing over everything, swallowing all the difficulties up in His victory train. I see

His Word going out to all the languages of the world, part of the tsunami of His growing kingdom, flowing through the earth, filling it with His goodness and glory, its powerful waves claiming the whole of creation for Christ.

I see Jesus reigning in majesty as rightful King over all mankind, whom He purchased at the cross with His blood. The moment His Son died and rose again, God took the boulder of His grace and threw it into the sea of creation, resulting in a tidal wave that would inundate the world. That wave continues to spread today, leaving no corner of our world untouched. Its living waters will indeed fill the whole earth as the waters cover the sea. "For it is the God who commanded light to shine out of darkness, who has shone in our hearts to give the light of the knowledge of the glory of God in the face of Jesus Christ" (2 Cor. 4:6).

And I see beyond this to when time ends and innumerable voices sing praises before the throne of the Most High, the Almighty God, the King of Kings and Lord of Lords, for all eternity. And when I listen, I hear Bakwé voices among them. I see God in glorious majesty, surrounded by His people—people from every tribe, tongue, and nation, now made immortal, bought by the blood of Jesus Christ. I see creation renewed, and nature no longer bound by the curse, but changed and perfected, the way it was meant to be, everything that was so wrong before now made right.

All this I see written in the Holy Book that is *sharper than any two-edged sword*—the Word of God, the Bible.

Epilogue

WHEN WE WERE STILL IN THE THICK OF our own troubles with the war and my deteriorating health, Hans dreamed that he was back in Ivory Coast again:

> We were standing on a grassy hillside with a sunset lighting the sky. We descended into a tunnel of bushes that gleamed with light; their white-tipped leaves shone with radiance.
>
> Janvier and Moise met us on the other end and welcomed us back home. We went to inspect our property and came to the old banana grove, the ancient ones that were too shaded to give much fruit. I ran to them and felt their cool, shiny stalks in my hand. To my astonishment, they were full

of fruit, with not one drooping or brown leaf. Amazed, I wandered out into the sunlight to the orange tree. It wasn't diseased or stunted, as it always had been, and it didn't have thorns as orange trees normally do. It was the essence of what an orange tree should be—an orange tree perfected. As I marveled, I looked over to where our mango tree stood with the four hammocks attached to the trunk. The mango tree had large, ripe mangos instead of the usual few scrub ones unfit to eat. Its laden branches bowed in magnificence!

I looked underneath the tree, and there was one of our favorite hens scratching in the leaves with all her chicks. I ran to the hen, and instead of attacking me like she always did, she brought her chicks for me to pick up. I stood in great confusion. Now I remembered! This hen was dead! A cobra killed her years ago. How could she be alive? Why were those banana trees strangely beautiful? Why was the orange tree in full health with no thorns? Why were there mangos on a tree that rarely bore fruit, and why was all our property shining with color as if it was suddenly, for the first time, very real?

I looked at the sky. It wasn't the typical hazy sky, but a rich blue, intensely deep and clear. Startled, I looked over at our ponds and saw the two ponds were joined together into one grand pond. The water was so clean that you could see sparkling rocks at the bottom and fish swimming in its cool waters.

The most amazing thing of all was a beautiful waterfall cascading into the pond from the sky! I thought to myself, "This can't be our property. Why is that hen alive? Why are things so changed?" In consternation, I shouted out to you, asking you where I was, because this place was not our property in the village!

I woke up, and it dawned on me that I had not been dreaming of our old home, but of *Home*...the way it should be where life is more real than it ever could be on earth, where we have stepped out of the reflection and into the real world.

To understand God's story is to realize there will be an end to our sufferings, and the end will be *glorious*. Look past the current dismal hill of trial to the glorious mountain beyond. In that place, there is no more death, nor sorrow, nor crying because God has swallowed it all up in victory. Even the memory of the trials we suffer on earth will fade away, although for now they are part of God's plan to prepare us for this place.

> For You cast me into the deep,
> Into the heart of the seas,

And the floods surrounded me;
All Your billows and Your waves passed over me.
Then I said, "I have been cast out of Your sight;
Yet I will look again toward Your holy temple."
. . . .
When my soul fainted within me,
I remembered the Lord;
And my prayer went up to You,
Into Your holy temple.

Those who regard worthless idols
Forsake their own Mercy.
But I will sacrifice to You
With the voice of thanksgiving;
I will pay what I have vowed.
Salvation is of the LORD. (Jonah 2:3–4, 7–9)

This book of our particular trials and how God worked through them to accomplish His purposes is just a drop in the ocean of what He is doing with His children throughout the world and throughout history. He is using all our situations and hardships to accomplish His glorious purposes. Nothing is ever wasted in His hands.

> When we shall come home and enter to the possession of our Brother's fair kingdom, and when our heads shall find the weight of the eternal crown of

glory, and when we shall look back to pains and sufferings; then shall we see life and sorrow to be less than one step or stride from a prison to glory; and that our little inch of time suffering is not worthy of our first night's welcome home to heaven.
(Samuel Rutherford)

Appendix

Three Life Stories

> So shall My word be that goes forth from My
>   mouth;
> It shall not return to Me void,
> But it shall accomplish what I please,
> And it shall prosper in the thing for which I sent
>   it. (Isa. 55:11)

THESE ARE THE PERSONAL STORIES OF three African men and how God used trials to accomplish His purposes in their lives.

THE CHIEF'S STORY: HOW ONE DEATH IMPACTED AN ENTIRE REGION

While we were on furlough one year, we heard that Yahou Francois, the chief of our village, had become a Christian. We were delighted. Csaba was hopeful that more Bakwé would follow, because there had been so few conversions up to that point. Then, to our joy, the chief's wife also became a Christian. Both these pieces of news were met with skepticism by the villagers; they watched to see if the spirits would take action against the couple since the chief had given up his fetishes.

Two years later, the chief was standing off to the side of the main road with several other people when a vehicle careened off the road, hitting only the chief. He was rushed to the nearest town for medical treatment but died from his injuries. We were shocked: a Bakwé leader had finally converted, and God had taken him! Yet this was not all. Not long after, his wife was in a bus traveling to town when a lightning bolt struck the vehicle, and only she was killed.

The village was thrown into an uproar. When Csaba heard about it, he felt sick, knowing exactly what the villagers would be thinking—the chief and his wife had given up their animistic beliefs, and the spirits had killed them for it. Csaba wondered what God was doing; this seemed like such a defeat.

Then Csaba began to understand. Since the chief and his wife were Christians, the church handled their funerals.

And because the chief was a very important man, people came from all over Bakwé land and stayed for days until his funeral was over, per Bakwé custom. The church preached the gospel to a "captive" audience during that time.

Years later, we heard reports of new evangelical churches popping up all over Bakwé territory. People were more open to hearing the gospel, though they had been so resistant before. The seeds were probably sown at the chief's funeral, and this was the fruit. Whereas Csaba had his sights only on one village, God had plans for the whole region.

DÉSIRÉ: A REJECTED BOY FINDS WHAT REALLY MATTERS

Désiré was essentially abandoned by his father when he was a child. In a fit of anger, his father threw his mother and her two sons out of his home. Désiré and his brother came to live in our village. Along with Janvier, our family tried to help them since they were very poor. Désiré remembers sitting at our table and listening to the Bible being read out loud after meals. He didn't understand English at the time, but he saw a difference in our lives and took note that we were Christians.

Since the Bakwé translation wasn't finished yet, Csaba challenged Désiré to read through the Bible in French. Désiré took up the challenge and felt the Word of God working in his heart, leading him to Christ.

When his father found that he had become a Christian, he got angry and told Désiré to leave the church. Désiré refused, so his father ceased all communication with him. Sometime later, his mother died. Since he was practically an orphan, he sought out his father again. His father said that he regretted cutting communication with him but hadn't known how to ask for him to come back. When his father also died, Désiré found out that the rest of his siblings had taken the inheritance and left him nothing.

By then, Désiré had become an apprentice tailor, and I often employed him to make our family's clothes. He said that my persistence in having him redo things helped him to fine-tune his skills. Once he finished his apprenticeship, we helped him start his own business in the market town of Méadji. His business became successful but suffered when he was negligent in his work and not consistent with his hours.

Csaba told him that, as a Christian, he needed to work hard and be dependable. Désiré listened, but it didn't sink in. He married and moved to Burkina Faso, partly because his family had disinherited him, and partly because he wanted to go to tailoring school. He left his wife in Ivory Coast and planned to send for her later. He realized he could have strayed from God at that point since his focus was on other things, but in God's grace he didn't. He found a good church in Burkina Faso, got serious about his faith, and started applying himself to both it and his work with diligence.

While he was in tailoring school, Désiré worked hard at his own tailoring business on the side and was soon able to bring his wife to join him. He even won a tailoring prize for his quality work. At the same time, he went to night school to continue his education (which had stopped at the fifth grade), working hard and finishing at the top of his class. After tailoring school, he went on to Bible school with the intention of becoming a pastor.

After Bible school, Désiré moved back to Ivory Coast. His denomination wanted him to serve at a church in Abidjan, but there were few Bakwé there. He felt a calling to reach his own people, so he was appointed to plant a church in the Bakwé village of Krohon. He was active in ministry and evangelism there. Since the new church couldn't support him financially, he set up a tailor shop. Much later, Désiré went on to get training in Bible translation, and he is now part of the team helping Csaba with the Bakwé Old Testament translation.

Désiré gives glory to God for who he has become through His love and grace that worked in him and for God's mercy in bringing him to our village and to the Bible. Csaba told him that real success is walking with the Lord, and Désiré has been faithful to do just that. Désiré told us with deep thankfulness, "I wouldn't be who I am if I hadn't gone through all that I did. If I had not been rejected by my father, I would not have come to this village and come to know Jesus Christ." He had found what really mattered.

YEGBÉ: HOW GOD USED A SMALL BOY TO BRING THE GOSPEL TO THE MWAN PEOPLE

Yegbé Antoine is the translation consultant who helped Csaba finish the New Testament. Even though he is not Bakwé, his story is a fascinating tale of how God used an untimely death to bring His Word to the Mwan people of central Ivory Coast.

The Mwan are traditional animists with a heavy Muslim influence. When Yegbé was young, a Muslim imam told his father, "Your son is smart. Will you give him to me to attend Koranic school?" His father said yes, and Yegbé was enrolled in the school and forced to recite the Koran in Arabic without understanding a word of it. One day, when he couldn't pronounce one of the verses correctly, the master pinched his ear so hard that blood flowed. "It is a sin not to recount this perfectly!" he warned Yegbé.

Yegbé ran home and told his father he never wanted to go back to Koranic school again; he wanted to go to the government school, which was taught in French. His father said that his brother was already in French school and that he could not afford to pay for another. Yegbé went and talked to the director of the French school, who approached Yegbé's father to find out why his son couldn't attend. Under pressure from the director, his father changed his mind and let him enroll.

After finishing at that school, Yegbé commuted to a secondary school in a neighboring town. During his first year, a boy took a cap that Yegbé had borrowed from his tutor. Yegbé tried to get it back, but the boy wouldn't give it, so Yegbé slapped him in the face. When Yegbé reported the missing cap to the officials, they forced the boy to give it back to him. As he did, the boy cursed him, saying, "Tomorrow you won't be able to even use that hand, because I belong to the most dreadful tribe." This boy was from an ethnic group purported to have magical powers.

The next day, Yegbé's hand was fine, but his leg felt itchy. Then it swelled up so badly that he went back to his village, where his father took him to a fetish priest. The priest said that he had been mystically poisoned by sorcery and gave Yegbé two fetish belts for protection. He also gave him a potion in a clay jar. Yegbé's leg got a little better, and he returned to school, but after several months the swelling came back.

Around this time, Yegbé decided to visit his older brother, who was a Christian. Yegbé made sure to tell him he didn't want to talk about Jesus.

Even though his brother didn't talk about Jesus, the radio *did*. One day, Yegbé was listening to a Christian broadcast when the preacher said, "There are those of you who are suffering from a disease which is not getting better. Maybe you have tried other means, like a fetisher, but it hasn't done any good. Give that all up and turn to Jesus, who can heal you."

The next morning, Yegbé asked his brother to pray for him to become a Christian. His brother said, "*You?* A

Christian? If this is real, you pray to Him yourself. Repent of your sins and give your life to Jesus."

Yegbé said, "I am afraid to pray. I am such a sinner and have spoken against this Christ. I am afraid He will beat me for how I have cursed Him."

His brother said, "Jesus will not do that. He loves you and will listen. Now go to Him."

Yegbé knelt down, closed his eyes, and prayed, "Jesus, I am coming to You to pardon me. I am giving myself to You today, so pardon all that I have done against You. I am giving my fetishes to you, so free me, and I will be Your servant."

Then he wrapped his fetishes in a cloth and threw them away. He felt as if a heavy burden had fallen from him. In the evening, the pain in his leg eased, followed by a decrease in swelling until he could put his shoes on again. He ran to his brother and told him he was healed.

After this, Yegbé read his Bible and went to church on a regular basis. God's power was at work, strengthening him for the next big test.

School resumed in September, and Yegbé preached to his fellow students so much that he earned the nickname *the evangelist*. But one night people arrived at his house with a hearse. Yegbé went outside and found all his brother's friends gathered around. He was told that his brother had been killed in a motorcycle accident. They had come to take him with them for the funeral.

After the burial, the village elders blamed Christianity for his brother's death. They knew Yegbé was also a Christian, so they called a meeting and placed Yegbé in the middle of the circle.

"Your brother was killed by one of the spirits," they said.

Yegbé responded, "No, he was called back into the kingdom of His God. It was a natural death and not from sorcery."

"You must abandon your faith!"

"I can't do this."

"Jesus killed your brother. If you don't stop following Him, you will be killed, too."

Yegbé responded again, "I am not afraid. My life is in the hands of my God."

As the elders were saying these things, Yegbé turned to his father. "You are my father, and I love you, but I can't stop believing in Jesus."

The elders continued to taunt him. "Jesus killed your brother, so who is going to pay for your school now?" His brother had been covering his tuition at secondary school.

Yegbé replied, "My father, you know that I love you. But even if you don't pay for my school supplies, I am convinced that Jesus will provide."

The elders yelled in anger, "And maybe Jesus will come down from heaven to do this! You are just a small boy. What do you know?"

They stripped off Yegbé's shirt and tied his hands behind his back. Then they yelled threats at him, saying they would beat him if he didn't recant his faith.

Yegbé replied, "Jesus doesn't kill people, but loves them. What you are doing is under the power of Satan. You don't understand that God loves you, too."

They continued to threaten him. One of his uncles shouted, "You are going to die!" and fired his gun right over Yegbé's head.

Yegbé remained calm, and in his heart said, "You are vanquished in Jesus' name!"

The elders talked amongst themselves and decided that they should punish Yegbé by rubbing hot peppers in his eyes. Before they could do this, another of his uncles said, "This boy is stubborn. He will never stop following Jesus. Even if you put pepper in his eyes, he won't give in, so we might as well disown him."

They chased him out of the meeting, and he went back to his house. His parents said he was a shame to them because he wouldn't listen to the elders. None of the other village children were allowed to speak to him. Yet he persevered in his faith.

One day, Yegbé's aunt overheard one of his uncles talking to himself as he walked by, saying, "When I pass in front of him to attack him, there is a man there blocking the way. When I pass behind him there is a man there, too, like a guard protecting him. When I try to kill him from the side, there is that guard again. If it had not been for this Jesus, I would have finished him long ago! One day I'll find a way to kill him!"

That aunt told Yegbé's mother what she had heard. His mother told his father, "They are going to kill him! I have never taken part in your sorceries. Your sorcerers killed my other son, and now you are going to kill this son, too? I oppose what you are doing!"

Just then, Yegbé came into the room. "Who are you talking about?"

"I am talking about you, my son."

Yegbé responded, "Mother don't worry; nobody is going to hurt me. Jesus will protect me. You don't need to take my defense. My defender is not a human being."

His mother got upset because she thought he was being ungrateful. In a rage, she took up a piece of wood and tried to hit him, but missed. He ran out of the house as his mother yelled, "Where was your Jesus when my other son was killed?"

Yegbé went back to school, and God did provide for him. One of the local missionaries asked her supporters for help with his school funds since he was known to be a hard worker and a good student. This support lasted through high school, and Yegbé worked hard on the side to supplement it. After graduation, he got a scholarship and became the first boy from his village to attend university. God had big plans for the boy that the village rejected.

Before his brother's death, Yegbé had attended a youth camp. There, a Wycliffe translator named Thomas Bearth set up a meeting with Yegbé's brother, who had expressed an interest in translation. Yegbé went with his brother to the meeting. In a recorded interview, Thomas asked if they wanted a Bible translation in Mwan, and they both said yes.

In 1974, Margrit Boli, another Wycliffe translator, was conducting a language survey to see if a translation into Mwan was needed or if the Mwan people could use an existing translation of a similar language. She listened to the recording of that interview and heard Yegbé saying how he wanted a translation in his language. Margrit tracked Yegbé down and invited him to a workshop on the principles of Bible translation. After attending the workshop, Yegbé did his first translation—a draft of the Gospel of Mark in Mwan. The next year, he translated Philippians. During this time, he finished university. Then Yegbé went to Kenya to do a master's program in translation; when he left for Kenya, he had already finished a first draft of the entire New Testament.

One day, his mother got sick, and Christians preached the gospel to her. She was receptive and became a true believer before she died. His father also heard the gospel at that time but did not become a Christian. After Yegbé's wedding eight years later, his father saw God's blessings in action in the way He provided for Yegbé, so he gave his life to Christ, along with Yegbé's older and younger brothers. But there was still no church in the Mwan region to help these new Christians.

Then Yegbé's father became ill and died. His body was brought back to the village, and a tape of the Gospel of Mark in Mwan was played at the funeral. This was instrumental in causing the first Mwan church to be born. The tape went out to eight other villages, and in each village a church was planted. Yegbé had the Mwan New Testament published, and at the dedication ceremony on August 4, 2012, all the New Testaments that they had printed were sold.

www.ingramcontent.com/pod-product-compliance
Lightning Source LLC
Chambersburg PA
CBHW070647120526
44590CB00013BA/858